Social Issues
in Literature

Workers' Rights in Upton Sinclair's *The Jungle*

Other Books in the Social Issues in Literature Series:

Social Issues
in Literature

Workers' Rights in Upton Sinclair's *The Jungle*

Gary Wiener, Book Editor

GREENHAVEN PRESS
A part of Gale, Cengage Learning

GALE
CENGAGE Learning™

Detroit • New York • San Francisco • New Haven, Conn • Waterville, Maine • London

GALE
CENGAGE Learning™

Christine Nasso, *Publisher*
Elizabeth Des Chenes, *Managing Editor*

© 2008 Greenhaven Press, a part of Gale, Cengage Learning

Gale and Greenhaven Press are registered trademarks used herein under license.

For more information, contact:
Greenhaven Press
27500 Drake Rd.
Farmington Hills, MI 48331-3535
Or you can visit our Internet site at gale.cengage.com

For product information and technology assistance, contact us at

Gale Customer Support, 1-800-877-4253
For permission to use material from this text or product, submit all requests online at www.cengage.com/permissions

Further permissions questions can be emailed to permissionrequest@cengage.com

Articles in Greenhaven Press anthologies are often edited for length to meet page requirements. In addition, original titles of these works are changed to clearly present the main thesis and to explicitly indicate the author's opinion. Every effort is made to ensure that Greenhaven Press accurately reflects the original intent of the authors. Every effort has been made to trace the owners of copyrighted material.

Cover image © The Library of Congress.

LIBRARY OF CONGRESS CATALOGING-IN-PUBLICATION DATA

Workers' rights in Upton Sinclair's The jungle / Gary Wiener, book editor.
   p. cm. -- (Social issues in literature)
  Includes bibliographical references and index.
  ISBN-13: 978-0-7377-4066-0 (hbk.)
  ISBN-13: 978-0-7377-4067-7 (pbk.)
  1. Sinclair, Upton, 1878-1968. Jungle. 2. Sinclair, Upton, 1878-1968--Political and social views. 3. Employee rights in literature. 4. Industrial relations in literature. 5. Employee rights--United States. 6. Industrial relations--United States. I. Wiener, Gary.
  PS3537.I85J988 2008
  813'.52--dc22
                                     2008000796

Printed in the United States of America
2 3 4 5 6 7 12 11 10 09

Contents

Lured by the promise of good jobs and a better life, millions of Russians immigrated to the United States. But American capitalism rewarded the immoral and unscrupulous man instead of the hard-working one.

Chapter 3: Contemporary Perspectives on Workers' Rights

Introduction

Upton Sinclair wrote *The Jungle* with one goal in mind: to improve working conditions for those who labored as "wage slaves." This objective is made absolutely clear on the very first page of the novel, which bears the dedication "To the Workingmen of America." Ironically, *The Jungle* did little to improve workers' rights. Instead, readers focused on a narrow selection of passages that graphically described the unsanitary conditions in meatpacking plants. These passages were so realistic, riveting, and grotesque that they made readers, including President Theodore Roosevelt, sick to their stomachs. In 1906, legislation was passed to ensure more sanitary conditions in the plants, but nothing similar was done to improve the horrendous working conditions of the workers themselves. "I aimed at the public's heart," Sinclair famously said, "and by accident hit it in the stomach."

It was not for lack of trying that *The Jungle* never became "the *Uncle Tom's Cabin* of wage-slavery," as Sinclair had intended. Sinclair's tale of the rise and fall and ultimate conversion to socialism of his hero, the Lithuanian immigrant, Jurgis Rudkus, is packed with scenes of worker abuse at the hands of unethical employers, lawyers, politicians, saloon keepers, and real estate agents. The harrowing tale of Jurgis's family is so drenched with pathos that it is difficult to imagine how his life can possibly get worse—until it does. In the course of the novel, Jurgis loses his home, his wife and her unborn child, his father, other assorted relatives (including children), and his firstborn son. All of these losses stem from the Rudkuses' predicament as wage slaves in America, who must work excessively long hours just to meet the basic requirements of living, and whose paltry wages often cannot even provide for these basic needs.

Sinclair was writing from experience. Living hand-to-mouth in a miserable cabin near Princeton, New Jersey, he wrote *The Jungle* out of solidarity with all of those who could not earn a living wage:

> I wrote with tears and anguish, pouring into the pages all that pain which life had meant to me. Externally the story had to do with a family of stockyard workers, but internally it was the story of my own family. Did I wish to know how the poor suffered in winter time in Chicago? I only had to recall the previous winter in the cabin, when we had only cotton blankets, and had rags on top of us. It was the same with hunger, with illness, with fear. Our little boy was down with pneumonia that winter, and nearly died, and the grief of that went into the book.

With the publication of *The Jungle*, and the public outcry that followed, Sinclair became famous. He attempted to use that fame to improve workers' rights and promote his preferred form of government, democratic socialism, as an antidote to the *laissez-faire* capitalism that trapped low-income workers into a life of poverty. In these endeavors, he was unsuccessful. Having been invited to lunch with President Roosevelt, Sinclair tried to use this proximity to power to his advantage, but Roosevelt, who had eaten tainted meat as a soldier in the Spanish-American War, was, like the rest of America, more interested in food safety than working conditions. Sinclair continued to badger him about workers' rights and socialism after this meeting, and Roosevelt grew more distant as he did. The relationship grew strained, as evidenced by Roosevelt's subsequent comments. After enduring a barrage of the author's urgent letters, Roosevelt suggested to Sinclair's publisher, "Tell Sinclair to go home and let me run the country for a while." In a letter to William Allen White in July 1906, Roosevelt wrote of Sinclair: "I have an utter contempt for him. He is hysterical, unbalanced, and untruthful. Three-fourths of the things he said were absolute falsehoods. For some of the remainder there was only a basis of truth." Roosevelt even coined the term *muckraker* to describe what Sinclair and similar writers were doing to expose America's problems. Roosevelt did not mean the term kindly, and when he ultimately signed the 1906 Pure Food and Drug Act, made no mention of Upton Sinclair.

Nevertheless, for the rest of his life Sinclair persevered in his quixotic quest to end poverty and improve workers' lives. He continued to write novels, such as *The Moneychangers* and *Oil!*, which attacked capitalism and exposed the sordid underworld of American business. With his earnings from *The Jungle*, he founded a doomed utopian community called Helicon Hall (which later burned down) and the Intercollegiate Socialist Society to encourage socialism on college campuses. He moved to California in 1915 and won the Democratic primary for governor of that state in 1934. Campaigning during the Great Depression on his EPIC (End Poverty in California) platform, he narrowly lost his bid for governor to the Republican candidate, Frank Merriam.

Despite all of his failures, Sinclair remains an American icon, dedicated to social justice. Though he had ultimately been rejected by Roosevelt, two later presidents paid him high tribute. On Sinclair's eightieth birthday, Harry Truman wrote that Sinclair "has been a burr under the saddle of people who cannot appreciate what working men have to contend with." In 1967, Lyndon Johnson invited Sinclair to the White House to witness the signing of the Wholesale Meat Act, which strengthened some of the provisions of the earlier Pure Food and Drug Act.

Sinclair wrote over ninety books during his long career, but he will be remembered for just one, *The Jungle*. The articles that follow place *The Jungle* in the context of workers' rights, suggesting why the novel became an instant *cause célèbre* in American literary, social, and political circles. These articles reveal, above all, that the debate concerning American business practices that Sinclair began in 1906 has not ceased in the one hundred–plus years since *The Jungle*'s publication.

Chronology

1878

Upton Beall Sinclair Jr. is born September 20 in Baltimore, Maryland.

1888

Sinclair moves with his family to New York.

1892

Sinclair enrolls in the College of the City of New York.

1897

Sinclair writes potboilers to finance his education.

1900

Sinclair marries Meta H. Fuller.

1906

The Jungle is published. Sinclair founds Helicon Hall. The Pure Food and Drug Act becomes law.

1907

The Metropolis and *The Moneychangers* are published; fire destroys Helicon Hall.

1911

Love's Pilgrimage is published.

1912

Sinclair and Meta divorce.

1913

Sinclair marries Mary Craig Kimbrough.

1915
Sinclair moves to California.

1917
King Coal is published; Sinclair resigns from the Socialist Party.

1919
Jimmie Higgins is published.

1920
The Brass Check and *100%* are published.

1923
The Goose-Step is published.

1924
The Goslings is published.

1925
Mammonart is published.

1927
Oil! is published.

1928
Boston is published.

1934
Sinclair wins the Democratic primary for governor of California but loses the general election.

1935
I, Candidate for Governor is published.

1936
Co-op is published.

1937
The Flivver King is published.

1940
World's End, the first book in the Lanny Budd series of novels, is published.

1941
Between Two Worlds is published.

1942
Dragon's Teeth is published.

1943
Sinclair wins the Pulitzer Prize for *Dragon's Teeth*.

1944
Presidential Agent is published.

1945
Dragon Harvest is published.

1946
A World to Win is published.

1947
Presidential Mission is published.

1953
The Return of Lanny Budd is published.

1956
The Cup of Fury is published.

1957
Southern Belle, by Sinclair's wife Mary, is published.

1960

My Lifetime in Letters is published.

1961

Mary Craig Sinclair dies on April 26; Sinclair marries May Hard on October 15.

1962

The Autobiography of Upton Sinclair is published.

1967

Sinclair's third wife, May Hard Sinclair, dies.

1968

Sinclair dies on November 25 in New Jersey.

Social Issues
in Literature

CHAPTER 1

Background on
Upton Sinclair

The Life of Upton Sinclair

William A. Bloodworth

William A. Bloodworth has taught at East Carolina University and has served as president of Augusta State University. He is the author of the book Upton Sinclair.

More concerned with ideas than the form or style of a novel, Upton Sinclair was an idealist whose interest in social justice drove his writing career and even led to an unsuccessful run for governor of California. Sinclair was born into poverty and began writing pulp fiction in order to pay for college. These early writings paved the way for The Jungle, *the novel that would make him famous overnight. But much of his life after the publication of his masterwork was anticlimactic, and among his many works of fiction, few have lasting literary value. Thus, Sinclair's literary reputation declined significantly after World War II. One of the ironies of his career was that for a man who was essentially a gentle soul he wrote some of the most aggressive and confrontational fiction of the twentieth century.*

Upton Sinclair was a writer whose main concerns were politics and economics. His ideas about literature—his own, written over more than six decades, and that of others—were inseparable from his dreams of social justice. Consequently, the great majority of his books, fiction as well as nonfiction, were written as specific means to specific ends. Since the essential purpose of literature, for Sinclair, was the betterment of human conditions, he was a muckraker [a writer who exposes corruption], a propagandist, an interpreter of socialism and a critic of capitalism, a novelist more concerned with content than form, a journalistic chronicler of his times rather than an enduring artist. Since World War II, his literary

William A. Bloodworth, "Upton Sinclair," *Dictionary of Literary Biography, Volume 9: American Novelists, 1910–1945*, Belmont, CA: Gale, 1981, pp. 25–32. Reproduced by permission of Gale, a part of Cengage Learning.

reputation has declined. Yet *The Jungle* (1906) is one of the best known and most historically significant of American novels, and Sinclair himself remains an important figure in American political and cultural history.

Always a Localist

Although it is possible to do justice to several of Sinclair's novels by examining them as individual literary works—particularly in the cases of *The Jungle* and *Oil!* (1927)—there are equally significant things to be learned by studying Sinclair's entire career and noting in it the interrelationships among his life, his times, and his writings. His single-minded intensity is the unifying feature; Sinclair was always the idealist—and the visionary—who agreed with [English poet Percy Bysshe] Shelley that writers are the unacknowledged legislators of the world, or at least should be, and who seldom doubted that his ideas and words would, if heeded, produce a better world. Beyond these surface attitudes, but never completely buried in his works, lie a number of contradictions and tensions. Sinclair was a person of essentially genteel and conservative upbringing who became a literary radical. Although he has often been seen as the champion of the oppressed, a novelist who wrote for and about the lowest working classes, many of his works have elitist tendencies. More than anything else though, he was a nineteenth-century idealist of initially romantic and even Nietzschean [after the German philosopher Friedrich Nietzsche] traits who chose to confront the hard facts of twentieth-century industrial life. His sense of certainty led him astray at times and prevented him from creating complex modern works of fiction, but he probably had a larger and more concrete influence on American life than most other novelists of the twentieth century.

Early Years

The origins of Sinclair's unique career lie in the circumstances of his childhood and adolescence: genteel cultural influences, poverty, idealism, ambition. He grew up in Baltimore and New York City as the only son of a ne'er-do-well salesman from a respected Virginia family. His mother was the daughter of a wealthy Baltimore family that presented a decided contrast to the usually shabby existence provided by his father. At the age of eighteen, while finishing up at the City College of New York [CCNY], Upton Beall Sinclair, Jr., began his writing career as the pseudonymous author of boys' adventure stories for Street and Smith, the leading American publisher of pulp fiction and dime novels. In embarking upon a career as a hack writer, Sinclair sought, with considerable success, to achieve economic independence from his alcoholic father. In four years he produced hundreds of stories whose techniques, especially *deus ex machina* plots [plots resolved by an artificial or improbable plot device] and two-dimensional characterizations, seem to have periodically insinuated themselves into his later works. During the latter three years of this unusual apprenticeship, following his graduation from CCNY, he also took courses, but no degree, from Columbia University. Among the subjects he felt himself drawn to were music, contemporary politics, and Romantic poetry. In the Romantic poets, especially Shelley, whom he studied under George Edward Woodberry, Sinclair found sufficient inspiration to abandon his career as a pulp writer and take up the production of serious literature.

Young Sinclair's first real literary efforts, between 1900 and 1904, were novels which took romantic idealism itself as their central subject. Read today, these works—*Springtime and Harvest* (1901), *Prince Hagen* (1903), *The Overman* (1907, written in 1902–1903), *The Journal of Arthur Stirling* (1903), and *A Captain of Industry* (1906, written in 1903)—seem immature and awkwardly pretentious. But they clearly show Sinclair groping toward a discovery of socialism. This discovery began with romantic idealism, passed through an exuberant fascination with Nietzsche and the possibilities of self, and emerged in a recognition that spirit and idealism have few chances in a world of corruption and oppression.

Sinclair's essential literary step toward socialism was the writing of *Manassas* (1904), a novel of the Civil War in which a young Southerner, Alan Montague, the son of a plantation owner, becomes a proponent of Abolition. Prior to writing this novel Sinclair had begun to learn about the socialist movement from prominent socialists in New York. His writing an abolitionist novel suggested that he had broken with his own Southern roots and was now prepared to adopt a radical stance toward social problems. Furthermore, the form of *Manassas*, in which Alan Montague is present at many important events and meets a wide range of historical figures—including Jefferson Davis, Abraham Lincoln, Frederick Douglass, and John Brown—prefigures the structure of many of Sinclair's later novels, particularly the eleven-volume Lanny Budd series published between 1940 and 1953. *Manassas* is the best of his early novels, and its theme of idealistic opposition to an unjust society is *the* theme of Upton Sinclair.

The Jungle

Manassas also created the opportunity for *The Jungle* (1906) by convincing the editor of a radical paper to challenge Sinclair to write a novel treating the "wage slaves" of industry in a manner similar to the treatment of chattel slaves in *Manassas*. Thus, in the fall of 1904 Sinclair spent two months in the packing-plant district of Chicago, the scene of an unsuccessful strike against the packers several months earlier. He talked with workers and visited the packing plants both as an official tourist and, in disguise, as a worker. He saw enough corruption, filth, and poverty to make *The Jungle* a gripping, emotionally wrenching novel.

The exact nature of *The Jungle* lies somewhere between pure fiction and muckraking journalism on a formalistic scale, and somewhere between determinism [the concept that events

Upton Sinclair Hulton Archive/Getty Images

are inevitable] and reform on an ideological scale. It is the story of oppressive industrial conditions as they affect a Lithuanian family that comes to Chicago expecting to achieve the American dream. Instead, their life becomes a nightmare of toil, poverty, and death. Jurgis Rudkus, the leader of the family and Sinclair's version of a proletarian hero, not only sees his father, wife, and son die, but he is also brutalized by working conditions in the Chicago packing houses and exploited by corrupt politics fashioned by the "Beef Trust." The grim details of life in Packingtown, all drawn from Sinclair's own firsthand knowledge, are communicated with a raw stylistic energy quite appropriate to Sinclair's equally raw and violent subject matter.

The structure of the novel is complicated by Sinclair's attempt first to show how heartbreaking life could be for the industrial proletariat and then to depict socialism as the obvious way to improve that life. After Jurgis is reduced to extreme forms of degradation, becoming a hobo, a criminal, and even a strike-breaking scab, he stumbles into a socialist lecture. The lecture transforms his view of the world; he is virtually born again. But once this occurs, his role as protagonist in the narrative disappears, and the last few chapters of the novel are given over to socialist argument and analysis which Jurgis hears but does not generate. Instead, the statements, chiefly optimistic projections of a new world in the making, come from the mouths of articulate, educated, and even wealthy socialists. In the socialist ending of *The Jungle*—in contrast to the naturalistic narrative preceding it—the working class loses its voice.

In spite of these problems, *The Jungle* had, and still has, inestimable value as a powerful story depicting conditions and people that do not often appear in the pages of American literature. It both questions the American dream of success and demands that that dream be more inclusive and more rigorously transformed into economic reality.

Aftermath of *The Jungle*

For Sinclair himself, *The Jungle* virtually guaranteed that the rest of his career would be anticlimactic. The success of the novel, including its impact on legislation aimed at pure food and sanitary meat processing, was an act which Sinclair found difficult to follow. Between 1906 and 1914, at which time Sinclair was again drawn to a specific working class problem, his career took several directions. He organized a communal living experiment at Helicon Hall in New Jersey only to see the building burn down in March 1907. He wrote *The Industrial Republic* (1907), a nonfiction attempt to explain that socialism can be achieved by "a process as natural . . . as that by which a chick breaks out of its shell." The primary value of the book is its elucidation of the benevolent but naive spirit of pre-World War I American socialism. Seeking answers to personal problems, especially the breakup of his marriage, Sinclair began to live in several utopian communities. He wrote about diet and health, at times promoting fasting as a cure for a wide variety of diseases. All the while he continued to write novels. In 1908 he had *The Metropolis* and *The Moneychangers* published, the first a muckraking novel about upper-class New York society and an almost libelous story of high finance based rather obviously on the affairs of [business tycoon] J. P. Morgan; both are poor novels of good intentions in which Sinclair's obsessive hatred of wealth, corruption, and loose morals triumphs over his narrative skills. In 1910 he produced *Samuel the Seeker*, the story of a young man who tries on various religious and ideological identities before settling on socialism, even though socialism leaves him unconscious and bleeding, the victim of police brutality, at the end of the novel. While Sinclair was still in the midst of his physical and intellectual wandering, his strange, autobiographical novel entitled *Love's Pilgrimage* (1911) appeared, describing the painful circumstances of his first marriage to Meta Fuller. Written as personal justification for the divorce which Sinclair would eventually get in 1913, *Love's Pilgrimage* is a neo-feminist work arguing for the personal and intellectual needs of married women and showing candidly how one specific marriage, an initially idealistic union, had come apart under various pressures, including Sinclair's own confused and prudish attitudes toward sexuality. In 1913 Sinclair found himself interested in the subject of venereal disease, an interest which produced *Sylvia* (1913) and *Sylvia's Marriage* (1914), two novels detailing the life of a Virginia belle who marries for social status only to find that her upper-class husband is a carrier of gonorrhea.

Return to Workers' Rights

Three events helped bring Sinclair back to the kind of novel that he wrote best. One was his successful second marriage (to Mary Craig Kimbrough, a Southern belle with socialist sympathies). Another was his permanent residence in south-

ern California beginning around 1914. The third was an out-
break of industrial violence. Disturbed by the massacre of
striking coal miners and their families in Ludlow, Colorado, in
1914, Sinclair became involved in the labor and social problems of Western miners. Following the pattern that produced
The Jungle, he took a trip to Colorado, visited with miners,
talked to union officials, and, in describing his impressions of
Ludlow in an eloquent public letter to [business tycoon] John
D. Rockefeller (who owned many mines), said he felt "as if the
air I breathed were full of the smoke of powder and the scent
of human flesh; as if my ears were deafened with the screams
of women and children." The end result, three years later, was
King Coal (1917), his attempt to dramatize conditions in the
coal fields of the West. . . .

Following his work on *King Coal*, Sinclair was drawn into
the controversy surrounding America's entrance into World
War I. Feeling that German militarism represented a threat to
world peace, Sinclair temporarily parted ways with the American Socialist party, which opposed intervention. His act suggests a more flexible ideological attitude than that typically
demonstrated by American radicals in 1917. Sinclair's flexibility became just as evident in 1918 when he grew critical of
American military attempts to suppress the Bolshevik revolution. The war itself, and the political dilemma of American
socialists during the war, became the central concern of *Jimmie Higgins* (1919). . . .

In the 1920s Sinclair was one of the few pre-war socialists
who neither grew conservative nor became a member of the
Communist party and an advocate of revolution. One of the
main ways that he resisted the conservatism of the decade was
by printing and distributing his own books, thus avoiding
what he perceived as the unhealthy influence of big business
on commercial publishing. Consequently, from 1917 to the
early 1940s, Sinclair himself published virtually all of his

books and pamphlets; many of his major works, however, were also published simultaneously by New York publishers.

In the first years of the decade Sinclair wrote *100%* (1920) and *They Call Me Carpenter* (1922), novels of limited appeal that focus on false patriotism and violence among middle-class political reactionaries who, according to Sinclair, unwittingly acted out scenarios arranged by big business. These novels represent direct confrontation with the political atmosphere of the early 1920s, especially that associated with Attorney General [Mitchell] Palmer's "Red Raids" in 1919 and 1920. A similar confrontation occurs in a series of nonfiction analyses discussing the damaging influence of capitalism on various American institutions. These books, which Sinclair called his "Dead Hand" series—in contrast to Adam Smith's idea of a benevolent "Invisible Hand" at work in laissez-faire economics—include *The Profits of Religion* (1918); *The Brass Check* (1920), dealing with journalism; *The Goose-Step* (1923), dealing with education; and *Mammonart* (1925), dealing with art and literature. He also wrote tracts and plays, all critical of the normalcy which reigned in American politics in the 1920s. That Sinclair was essentially a novelist, however, and a novelist of a particular kind, became abundantly clear at the end of the decade when he produced *Oil!* (1927) and *Boston* (1928). . . .

Sidetracked by Politics

After his remarkable achievements in *Oil!* and *Boston*, Sinclair's career as a novelist faltered for some dozen years. Some of his literary failures in the early 1930s—especially *Mountain City* (1930) and *Roman Holiday* (1931)—resemble the weak muckraking fiction he produced immediately after *The Jungle*. Likewise, he again seemed to be sidetracked from the writing of genuinely realistic fiction focusing on class conflict and economic injustice; for instance, he wrote a book on mental telepathy entitled *Mental Radio* (1930) and a novel, *The Wet Parade* (1931), pleading moralistically for the retention of Prohibition.

But the chief reason for the decline of his career as a novelist in the 1930s was his involvement in electoral politics. In 1934, following the publication of a book entitled *I, Governor of California, and How I Ended Poverty* (1933), Sinclair became the Democratic candidate for governor in California. His campaign became known as the EPIC (End Poverty in California) campaign. Although Sinclair was unsuccessful in his bid for election, his appeal may have influenced the [Franklin D.] Roosevelt administration to pay more heed to left-wing demands. His experience in California politics is reflected in his novel *Co-op* (1936).

In the late 1930s Sinclair wrote his last novels about specific political situations. *The Flivver King* (1937) is a novelistic interpretation of Henry Ford; the book attacks Ford's employee practices and makes a case for the United Auto Workers. *No Pasaran!* (1937) is a short, quickly written story about the Spanish Civil War. *Little Steel* (1938) tells of an organization of steel companies determined to keep unions out of their industry.

At the end of the 1930s, with the world in turmoil, Sinclair looked backward to view the history of his times. Eventually he published eleven long, wide-ranging historical novels, all with the same central character, presenting the political history of the Western world from 1913 to 1950. The central character is Lanny Budd; the eleven novels are usually referred to as the Lanny Budd Series....

Later Years and Death

By the 1950s Sinclair had entered his eighth decade and had written millions of words and dozens of books. The semiretirement that he entered in the 1950s was certainly deserved, but it did not prevent him from producing a few more novels and his complete autobiography. Among the novels *Another Pamela* (1950) stands out as a clever effort at writing a modern version of Samuel Richardson's *Pamela* (1740–1742); in the 1950 version a rural California girl must first resist and then reform the promiscuous nephew of her wealthy employer. Also, *What Didymus Did* (1954) is of some interest because its story, essentially a fantasy in which a divinely inspired reformer unsuccessfully tries to transform human nature in Los Angeles, suggests that Sinclair had finally grown skeptical about the limits of reform. *The Autobiography of Upton Sinclair* (1962), which adds several chapters to *American Outpost*, the autobiography which Sinclair had published in 1932, is an important source of information about the Progressive era as well as about Sinclair.

When Sinclair died in 1968 most of the obituaries were generous in their praise. Some of them noted one of the main ironies of his career: that such an essentially gentle person, a man who exuded genteel innocence and probity in his personal life and who dabbled in such quaint matters as spiritualism and vegetarianism, could have written some of the most socially combative works in American fiction.

Sinclair Was an Idealist

David Denby

David Denby is a film critic who has written for the New Yorker. *He is the author of the book* Great Books.

Upton Sinclair was challenged by an editor to write a novel about the evils of wage slavery. The result of his firsthand research into the Chicago meatpacking industry was The Jungle, *a book so powerful that it influenced an entire nation's eating habits. Sinclair's subsequent idealistic schemes, such as forming a socialist living community, did not fare as well as his most famous novel, and he lost much of his windfall from* The Jungle. *He was not a great stylistic writer, and his characters, such as Jurgis, often lack emotional depth, but his power lay in his ability to create carefully detailed and powerful scenes that were shocking to read.* The Jungle *is one of those rare books that has influenced authors of later generations, and Sinclair's personal crusade for social justice, driven by his profound moral sense, makes him an enduring figure in American letters and history.*

[More than] a hundred years ago, Upton Sinclair, the muckraker and socialist, brought out "The Jungle," a sensationally grim exposé of the noisome squalors and dangers of the meatpacking industry. Dedicated to "the workingmen of America," the book became an overnight best-seller. At the White House, Theodore Roosevelt, who had watched soldiers die from eating rotten meat during the Spanish-American War, wrote a three-page appreciation and critique of the novel, and sent it to Sinclair with an invitation to visit him. "The Jungle" played a major role in pushing forward the Pure Food and Drug Act, which Roosevelt had long favored, and which was passed in June of 1906, marking a major expansion of federal regulatory power. The book's influence hit the dinner table as well: after a couple of years, meat consumption declined, and it was widely believed that Sinclair's book was the cause. By common consent among literary historians, only one American novel, before or since—Harriet Beecher Stowe's "Uncle Tom's Cabin"—has had so powerful an influence on practical affairs.

Sinclair Is Largely Forgotten

In 1906, Upton Sinclair was twenty-seven years old; he continued publishing for more than sixty years, a clattering typewriter that would not stop. No two scholars seem to agree on exactly how many books he wrote, but the number is above ninety, and his output, in addition to social-protest and historical novels, includes plays, screenplays, tracts, journalistic exposés, didactic dialogues, instructional manuals, and autobiographies. Sinclair spoke at rallies, joined strikes and protests, and repeatedly ran for political office; he sponsored [filmmaker] Sergei Eisenstein's epic unfinished documentary about Mexican Indians, "Que Viva Mexico." [American poet] Ezra Pound, who knew a thing or two about obsession, said that Sinclair was not a maniac but a "polymaniac." During many periods of his life, Sinclair's activities were widely discussed in the press, and in the eyes of some prominent contemporaries, including Albert Einstein, [German author] Thomas Mann, and [playwright George] Bernard Shaw, he was an invaluable guide to twentieth-century politics. To many people, however, he now seems remote and musty—the author of flaking volumes encountered in country book barns. Apart from "The Jungle," Sinclair's works have been largely forgotten, or perhaps simply mislaid, his name confused with that of [American novelist] Sinclair Lewis, the author of "Main Street," "Babbitt," and "Dodsworth."

Can anything in Sinclair's life and work still make a claim on us? At the moment, he's getting some of his old notice.

Paul Thomas Anderson, the director of "Boogie Nights" and "Magnolia," is adapting Sinclair's novel "Oil!" into a movie starring Daniel Day Lewis and titled "There Will Be Blood" (with luck, the title will be changed again). The novelist Chris Bachelder recently brought out a fantasia, "U.S.!," in which Sinclair, resurrected by diehard leftists, writes one terrible novel after another and is repeatedly slain by reactionaries—a bizarrely masochistic scheme that nevertheless catches Sinclair's jack-in-the-box energy. Reading two . . . biographies of Sinclair—one intimate and intellectually astute, *Radical Innocent: Upton Sinclair*, by Anthony Arthur, and one political and anecdotal, *Upton Sinclair and the Other American Century*, by Kevin Mattson—leaves one bewildered by the contradictory nature of his enthusiasms, and by the mixture of prescience and credulity in his temperament. What fuses these qualities, one finally realizes, is his dedication to an ethical notion of being an American. He was one of those professional citizens—like [American politician] William Jennings Bryan or [American author] H. L. Mencken or [American journalist] I. F. Stone—who took responsibility for the soul of the country but never (except for Bryan, briefly) held power. Through the years of America's century-long triumph, Sinclair was always mocking or scolding or keening for some unachievable national paradise. If he no longer seems original, it may be because he anticipated both our reforming high-mindedness and so many of our follies. . . .

Challenged to Write

In February of 1904, Sinclair finished "Manassas," a long novel about slavery and the Civil War, and, as he worked on the galleys, he read [German philosopher Karl] Marx and [Norwegian American sociologist and economist Thorstein] Veblen. [Socialist politician] Eugene V. Debs had formed the Socialist Party of America in 1901, and, in 1904, Sinclair joined up. In those early years of the century, socialism was a kind of militant humanism; Sinclair, like many socialists of the period, believed that the scramble for profits degraded relations between people. He approached socialism "as a moralist, not as a political theorist," Anthony Arthur writes. "Both his strengths and his weaknesses derived from his simplistic belief that all injustice stemmed from greed, whether for money or power." After "Manassas" was published, in the summer of 1904, the editor of a popular socialist magazine, *The Appeal to Reason*, challenged Sinclair to write a novel about "wage slavery."

At the time, livestock was among the largest industries in the country. In Chicago, companies like Armour and Swift owned acres of yards, pens, slaughterhouses, and packing plants. The filthy conditions in such places were an open secret, but the big companies, working together (the "Beef Trust"), bribed government inspectors, and exercised enough control over the local newspapers to avoid serious censure. The unions were weak and defenseless; the companies were able to replace rebellious workers from a constantly renewed pool of Central and Eastern European immigrants. In the pages of *The Appeal to Reason*, Sinclair had implored Chicago's meat workers, after an unsuccessful strike, to continue fighting, but he did it from a distance. Now he accepted the magazine's challenge and went to Chicago. He was twenty-six, a slender, pale young man with soft lips and liquid eyes. Zealous and excitable, he suffered from nervous tension, indigestion, and headaches. Away from his demanding and unhappy wife, however (she stayed behind in the cabin), he was content. He walked all over Chicago's more dismal neighborhoods, asking questions of workers, union organizers, settlement-house officials. And for days he wandered through the vast Armour facilities in shabby clothes, lunch bucket in hand. There was very little security at the plant. No one challenged this oddly inquiring worker.

The Jungle's Power

Sinclair built his narrative around a family of immigrant Lithuanians who settle in the stockyard area known as Packingtown. They have few illusions about wealth; they expect little more than employment and freedom from tsarist corruption. The broadbacked hero, Jurgis Rudkus, is a virtuous prole [worker] whose refrain, no matter what happens to him, is "I will work harder." At the stockyards, in a reverse anticipation of Henry Ford's production line, the cows are stunned with a sledgehammer, then hung up by one leg, beheaded, skinned, and so on—deconstructed as they move past one worker after another. Jurgis's job is to sweep the gutted slops into a hole in the floor, and at first he enjoys the hard, bloody labor. Within a few months, however, he is sore and disillusioned. The men are forced to perform at punishing speed; they are played off against one another by management and dismissed for any kind of rebellion or injury. The conditions, at times, are little short of torture:

> There was no heat upon the killing-beds; the men might exactly as well have worked out of doors all winter. For that matter, there was very little heat anywhere in the building, except in the cooking-rooms and such places—and it was the men who worked in these who ran the most risk of all, because whenever they had to pass to another room they had to go through ice-cold corridors, and sometimes with nothing on above the waist except a sleeveless undershirt. On the killing-beds you were apt to be covered with blood, and it would freeze solid; if you leaned against a pillar, you would freeze to that, and if you put your hand upon the blade of your knife, you would run a chance of leaving your skin on it. The men would tie up their feet in newspapers and old sacks, and these would be soaked in blood and frozen, and then soaked again, and so on, until by night-time a man would be walking on great lumps the size of the feet of an elephant.

The force of "The Jungle" can be suggested only by quoting it at length. Sinclair's prose is fluent and forward-moving, but he rarely writes an interesting phrase or discovers new weight or color in a word. He builds his effects through precise reporting and the remorseless piling up of detail; he was a master of the routines of physical labor and the gear-by-gear minutiae of industrial processes. In the meatpacking scenes, he holds his rhythm steady and lets the hideous facts do their work:

> There was never the least attention paid to what was cut up for sausage; there would come all the way back from Europe old sausage that had been rejected, and that was mouldy and white—it would be dosed with borax and glycerine, and dumped into the hoppers, and made over again for home consumption. There would be meat that had tumbled out on the floor, in the dirt and sawdust, where the workers had tramped and spit uncounted billions of consumption germs. There would be meat stored in great piles in rooms; and the water from leaky roofs would drip over it, and thousands of rats would race about on it. It was too dark in these storage places to see well, but a man could run his hand over these piles of meat and sweep off handfuls of the dried dung of rats. These rats were nuisances, and the packers would put poisoned bread out for them; they would die, and then rats, bread, and meat would go into the hoppers together.

It is the archetypal scene of industrial horror, an image that haunted the nation. If only Sinclair had possessed fiction-writing abilities equal to his ability to evoke squalor! One lurid catastrophe after another engulfs Jurgis Rudkus and his relatives—so many disasters that one suspects Sinclair outfitted the family with exactly those vulnerabilities which could be most grievously exploited by a brutal society. Jurgis is injured, loses his job, and takes to drink; his pretty young wife, who also works in the meatpacking district, is bullied by her foreman into becoming his mistress; their little boy drowns in the Packingtown muck. Jurgis breaks down, and Sinclair sends him reeling through the city, where he is brushed by "the hurrying throngs upon the streets, who were deaf to his entreaties, oblivious of his very existence—and savage and contemptuous when he forced himself upon them."

Sinclair's Characters Lack Depth

Available in many editions, "The Jungle" is still widely taught in schools and colleges. It has remained a moral text if not quite a literary one. You have only to read the first few chapters of "Germinal," [french novelist Émile] Zola's 1885 novel about French coal miners, to know what it feels like to be in the hands of a sensually and morally alive writer who establishes a tight pattern of significance rather than just laying on pages of atmosphere and calamity. Any kind of inwardness was beyond Sinclair: his characters, suffering without any gain in consciousness, remain mere names attached to depressing social conditions. Jurgis falls in with criminals and corrupt politicians, and then, suddenly, at a public meeting, he's electrified by a fervent voice: "They own not merely the labor of society, they have bought the governments; and everywhere they use their raped and stolen power to intrench themselves in their privileges." The book ends with Jurgis's rapid conversion to socialism and with an outpouring of blood-raising speeches inspired by the words of Eugene Debs. The last line of the novel is "CHICAGO WILL BE OURS!"

But Chicago didn't become "ours," which was something that Sinclair had trouble understanding. The shock created by "The Jungle" was extraordinary, but it didn't produce what Sinclair had hoped for—outrage over the exploitation of workers, and the first steps toward the defeat of capitalism. "I aimed at the public's heart, and by accident I hit it in the stomach," he later said, in perhaps his sole public witticism. Roosevelt brushed off the call for socialist revolution, and though he acted vigorously on contaminated food, his measures were neither as vigorous nor as comprehensive as Sinclair wanted. The writer, hanging around Washington, pestered the President with cables and protests, until Roosevelt, losing patience, wrote to Frank Doubleday, Sinclair's publisher, "Tell Sinclair to go home and let me run the country for a while."

Sinclair's Improvement Schemes

In the spring of 1906, at the time of the signing of the Pure Food and Drug Act, Sinclair was trying to build socialism on a small scale. His idea was that a select group of intellectuals and artists would band together and hire people to cook and clean for them and look after their children, leaving them free to work and exchange ideas. A refuge from commercial society, the enterprise was a descendant of the nineteenth-century colony Brook Farm, but without the emphasis on physical labor and schooling or the philosophical strength of Transcendentalism to hold it together. In November, 1906, Sinclair and his group jointly purchased a former boys' academy in Englewood, New Jersey, named Helicon Hall, after the mountain in Greek mythology whose rushing springs inspired the Muses. By the following March, eighty men and women (including writers, feminists, freelance philosophers) were living there, discussing [German philosopher Friedrich] Nietzsche and eating stunningly healthy dinners of beans, potatoes, turnips, prunes, and salt-free crackers known as "educators." College students swabbed the floors and tended the furnace (among them, dropping in for a laugh, was Sinclair Lewis, then a twenty-one-year-old Yale undergraduate). The New York papers, fascinated by the experiment, spoke of an atmosphere of "free love," which was probably a journalistic fantasy—Sinclair was hardly a bohemian. Helicon Hall became famous overnight and was visited by [American psychologist-philosopher] William James, [Lithuanian-born anarchist] Emma Goldman, and [American educator] John Dewey, who joined the board of directors. In March of 1907, however, the place mysteriously went up in flames, and Sinclair lost the funds he had sunk into it, including a good chunk of his proceeds from "The Jungle."

In the Helicon Hall affair, as on other occasions, Sinclair was plagued by the kind of comic misfortune that tends to befall those bent on improving themselves and others. He was skeptical of the morals of industrialists and newspaper publishers but receptive to the delusions of quacks. He had a weakness for nostrums and half-baked schemes (including his own). H. L. Mencken, with whom he had a joshing epistolary relationship for years, said of him, "He must suffer vicariously for the carnal ease of the rest of us. He must die daily that we may live in peace, corrupt and contented." This suggests a savior unable to save anyone, but failure never stopped Sinclair from preaching. In the Nineteen-twenties, when other American writers were excited by [Sigmund] Freud, [Irish novelist James] Joyce, and [Spanish painter Pablo] Picasso, or by Jazz, flappers, and booze, Sinclair was devoted to popular fads like dieting and homeopathy. At various times in his life, he gave himself over to programs of fasting, prolonged chewing, colonic cleansing, and other such methods of ideologically approved digestion. He practiced a kind of socialism of the body, its constituent parts rehabilitated along progressive lines—tennis for the heart and lungs, nuts and berries for the colon. . . .

The Jungle's Endurance

Most of Sinclair's fiction no doubt deserves to molder in the book barn. But the influence of "The Jungle" may still be seen in investigative journalism and in such books as Susan Sheehan's "A Welfare Mother" and Jonathan Kozol's "Rachel and Her Children," which use the resources of fiction to chronicle the lives of people who have dropped to the bottom of American society. Sinclair's ideas didn't go away, either. The union hall may be nearly empty, but his desire for an alternative world within American capitalism has borne fruit in such nonprofit organizations as food co-operatives, day-care centers, and public radio and television. His personal habits of non-stop opinionizing and self-serving rant find their natural heir in the blog. His austere citizenly dedication inspired the young [American activist and politician] Ralph Nader, who has acknowledged the debt. His obsession with health and physical culture prefigured our own. He was one of the great American squares, exasperating and tone-deaf his entire life. But an ethical man tugs at us from the grave more persistently than merely successful men, who have gone to a quieter form of rest.

Sinclair Was Defeated by the Forces He Attacked

Floyd Dell

Floyd Dell was a novelist, radical journalist, and socialist activist. He is the author of Upton Sinclair: A Study in Social Protest.

Sinclair's The Jungle *shook up the institution he attacked, the meatpacking trust, but not in the manner he intended. His novel had little practical effect toward ameliorating the chief problem it tackled, the rights of workers in Packingtown. Even as the novel was being read by millions, big business in America fought back with all of its power and influence. Sinclair's literary reputation was damaged in the battle. The era of muckraking had come to an end, and American audiences were no longer eager for heartrending tales of abused workers. Instead, public opinion turned back toward more cheerful literary fare. True to his nature, Sinclair refused to bow to pressure and continued writing muckraking tales that were not very good and did not sell well. But their lack of literary value was not the reason: had his novels been poor but fashionable, he would have maintained his standing in the literary community. It was not until after the First World War that he regained a measure of the respect that he had lost.*

In 1905 there began to appear, in a Socialist weekly, the *Appeal to Reason*, published in Girard, Kansas, a novel of the Chicago stockyards, by an almost altogether unknown writer: *The Jungle*, by Upton Sinclair. I can remember, as a boy of eighteen reading in my *Appeal* that first chapter describing the wedding party of Jurgis and Ona, and my delight in the rich,

Floyd Dell, *"The Jungle," Upton Sinclair: A Study in Social Protest*, New York: George H. Doran Company, 1927, pp. 104–120. Copyright © 1927 by Doubleday, a division of Random House, Inc. Copyright renewed 1954 by Floyd Dell. Used by permission of the publisher.

full-blooded humanity of that scene. It was the happy prelude to what was to be, as week after week the story unrolled itself, a tragic panorama of working-class life, true, terrible, and magnificent. . . .

The story was simple enough; it related the fortunes of a group of immigrants who lived and worked in the stockyards district—their struggle to get ahead, to own a home, to bring up their children decently, while all the time they are brutally exploited, preyed upon, robbed, outraged, by the unscrupulous forces which find in their poverty and ignorance and helplessness mere opportunities for enrichment. The group is crushed, one by one, in the struggle; the old men are thrown on the scrap-heap to starve, the women are drawn into prostitution to keep body and soul together, the children die; Jurgis himself goes to prison for smashing the face of a brutal boss, and when he comes out his little world had been destroyed as if by an earthquake—and he is left to wander, getting wisdom as he wanders, and coming at last to believe in a Socialist reconstruction of this hideous world. At every point the story is enriched by the most vivid and relentless realistic detail; one is immersed in the filth and stench and cruelty of the stockyards, and one feels the sublime human aspirations which even there burn unquenchably in humble hearts.

An Empathetic Audience

For a while the knowledge that a great new novelist had appeared in America was almost confined to the readers of that Socialist weekly—no small audience, however, for the "*Appeal* army" of enthusiastic subscription-getters had drummed up half a million readers for that publication. The first public, therefore, of this astonishing novel, was of farmers resting in stocking feet beside the stove of winter evenings, and of discontented workingmen in a thousand cities and towns—an audience which, whether rural or urban, understood the truths of human suffering which it so vividly portrayed. That was its first success—its recognition and acclaim by a proletarian audience. Then came recognition by fellow-writers, who heard of this strange and powerful novel being published in a Socialist weekly, and sent for back numbers. [Novelist] David Graham Phillips wrote to the author: "I never expected to read a serial. I am reading *The Jungle* and I should be afraid to trust myself to tell you how it affects me. It is a great work. I have a feeling that you yourself will be dazed some day by the excitement about it. It is impossible that such a power should not be felt. It is so simple, so true, so tragic, and so human. It is so eloquent, and yet so exact." And, of course, [American novelist] Jack London, his comrade in the Socialist movement did not fail to acclaim this achievement. "The *Uncle Tom's Cabin* of wage slavery" [referring to the famous antislavery novel by Harriet Beecher Stowe], he called it and with that legend on the jacket and in the advertisements it was brought before the general American public in book form in 1906. It was an immediate and enormous success. It became a "bestseller" in America, England and the British colonies. It was translated into seventeen languages, and the world became aware that industrial America in its toil, its misery and its hope had found a voice.

Sinclair's Charges Are Confirmed

But the literary sensation in America had already become secondary to the shock of its readers in learning of the conditions under which their meats were prepared in Packingtown, not as affecting the workers but as affecting their own health—for the story dealt incidentally with the use of condemned meat. The author later remarked that he had aimed at the public's heart and by accident had hit it in the stomach. His deepest concern had been with the fate of the workers, and he realized with bitterness that he had become a celebrity not because the public cared anything about the workers, but because it did not want to eat diseased meat.

The public was more or less prepared for such charges against the packers, on account of the "embalmed beef" scandal during the Spanish-American war. President [Theodore] Roosevelt, responding to a widespread popular demand, sent a commission to Chicago to make an investigation of conditions in Packingtown. This commission was assisted, at Sinclair's expense, by [American political organizer and writer] Ella Reeve Bloor, who had been familiar with conditions there and had helped him in his seven weeks' investigation preliminary to the writing of the novel; and the researches of this commission appear to have confirmed the chief charges made in the book.

Business Interests Fight Back

The young novelist accepted, as a Socialist, the opportunity which this situation provided for agitation. But the packers, and large business interests in general, were aroused, and all their power and influence was used to keep this agitation from reaching the public, and to represent the young agitator as an irresponsible sensation-monger. He set up a publicity bureau, worked twenty hours a day, wrote articles, sent telegrams, and gave interviews to roomfuls of reporters; but so thoroughly had the newspapers been mobilized by the business interests as a medium of defense that the publicity he actually achieved for the workers' cause was slight; and on the other hand, his own reputation, in genteel literary and critical circles, and among the public at large, was seriously damaged. In the course of these efforts, President Roosevelt said to him: "Mr. Sinclair, I have been in public life longer than you, and I will give you this bit of advice; if you pay any attention to what the newspapers say about you, you will have an unhappy time." He might have taken this as a warning that his temperament was not suited to public life, for he could not get used to being lied about in the newspapers; but he persisted in his efforts, and he did have a very "unhappy time."

Sinclair is pictured on the cover of Time magazine during his
1934 campaign for governor of California. In The Jungle and
other works, Sinclair advocated passionately for social and political reform. Time Inc./Time Life Pictures/Getty Images.

The Jungle Did Not Improve Working Conditions

Nothing in particular was done about the workers' conditions.
Even the President's meat-inspection law, as finally passed,
had, in the opinion of those behind it, all its teeth drawn
[pulled] first. Sinclair continued his attempt to agitate the
question, but the public had been reassured, and the effort
was futile. In [Sinclair's book] *The Brass Check*, where the
complete story of this period is told vividly, he says: "I look
back upon this campaign, to which I gave three years of brain

and soul sweat, and ask what I really accomplished." He had taken, he says, a few million dollars away from the Chicago packers, "giving them to the Junkers [land-owning aristocracy] of East Prussia [part of Germany], and to the Paris bankers who were backing enterprises to pack meat in the Argentine." He had also added a hundred thousand readers to the circulation of a popular magazine which speedily repudiated its early muck-raking habits and became a defender of big business; and he had made a fortune for his publishers, who immediately became conservative and devoted their profits from *The Jungle* to promote a kind of writing hostile to everything in which he believed. . . .

The Muckraking Era Climaxes

The Jungle was in fact the climax of a literary movement in America which had aroused the fear and anger of large business interests. The great middle-class reform movement, marked in the political field by the careers of [William Jennings] Bryan, Roosevelt and the earlier [Woodrow] Wilson, had produced an audience sympathetic to the telling of unpleasant truths about American political and business conditions. In the magazine field this was called "muck-raking"; there were sensational revelations of the inside workings of Wall Street by Tom Lawson, of municipal corruption by Lincoln Steffens, of Standard Oil history by Ida M. Tarbell, of Beef Trust finance by Ray Stannard Baker. In the fictional field there was a corresponding literature, written by such men as Robert Herrick, Frank Norris and David Graham Phillips. This literature has its social revolutionary fringe: Jack London was an avowed revolutionist, and such Socialist critics of society as W. J. Ghent, John Spargo, Robert Hunter, Charles Edward Russell and William English Walling, had a wide hearing. A professor named Thorstein Veblen had written a devastating book called *The Theory of the Leisure Class*, and phrases from it passed into general intellectual currency. These conditions were sufficiently alarming, in a country where every year, in one great industry or another, there was a bitter struggle between employers and men, in which bullets were the decisive factor. And now a young man, by writing a book, had put a great industry on the defensive before the whole public. It was necessary to tighten the grip of business upon the intellectual world. The newspapers were already well in hand; but there was a group of free magazines which were making money out of "muck-raking"—the very center of the intellectual rebellion. Big business struck at this group of free magazines, effectively, through the medium of advertising. The magazine policies were changed. Writers were called off from investigations of industrial conditions. An immense campaign of optimism was begun, and a cheerful outlook upon American industrial conditions was preached and made synonymous with patriotism. The writers for the most part changed with the times, and adapted their views to the new editorial demand; the others were silenced or discouraged. A few prominent radical journalists, unable to tell the truth any longer in the magazines, bought one of their own; but they, too, presently succumbed to the spirit of the times. . . . Sinclair quotes, in *The Brass Check*, the titles of some representative articles from a recent issue of that once-daring magazine: "How We Decide When to Raise a Man's Salary", "The Comic Side of Trouble", "Interesting People: A Wonderful Young Private Secretary", "From Prize-Fighter to Parson". . . .

Muckraking Loses Favor with Readers

The public, deprived of the intellectual stimulant of unpleasant truth before it had quite got used to it, was easily trained in more cheerful tastes. Those writers who sought to revive the art of muck-raking found themselves with an indifferent audience. "People aren't interested in that sort of thing any more." While as for fiction, the old genteel tradition reasserted itself, the standard of non-controversiality became identical with the standard of decency, and any author who dared to violate this standard ran the risk of finding himself removed in critical esteem beyond the pale of literary respectability. . . .

The stage of Upton Sinclair's literary career, immediately ensuing upon his immense celebrity as the author of *The Jungle*, falls within this period when "muck-raking" was being outlawed and editors and writers taught a lesson by those in control of American business. He was one of the few who dared to brave this Thermidorian [referring to the French revolt against the Reign of Terror] reaction, and he was chief of those to suffer from it. It is his temerity which explains the fact that his reputation in America as a novelist fell during that period to zero, or lower. He missed, by remaining a "muck-raker", his chance of regaining literary respectability. His next novel, *The Metropolis*, published in 1907, was an attack on New York society; and *The Money-changers*, published in 1908, was an exposé of Wall Street. Nor is this explanation to be discounted by the fact that *The Metropolis* and *The Money-changers* were not very good novels.

The point is worth laboring. Novels far inferior to those two would, in that period, have maintained Upton Sinclair in American critical esteem, if they had been of a different tendency; not to realize that is to be ignorant of American criticism and its fashions. It was the fashion to sneer at Upton Sinclair, and to accept the yellow-journal [disreputable newspapers] pictures of him, in which he was represented as a mere sensation-monger and fool to boot. Georg Brandes, generally accounted the world's greatest modern critic, was astonished at this American neglect of one of its greatest writers; on visiting this country in 1914, he took pains to say to the reporters who met him at the steamer that there were three American novelists whom he found worth reading, among these being Upton Sinclair. The statement, as it generally appeared in the press, referred only to Frank Norris and Jack London, omitting Upton Sinclair's name altogether. Doubtless it was naïvely regarded as incredible that anyone should really take this disreputable "muck-raker" seriously. . . . And it was not until a new rebellious literature and criticism emerged after the war, under the leadership of [American novelist] Sinclair Lewis and [American author] H. L. Mencken, that Upton Sinclair was again mentioned among American writers by any reputable native critic who was not a Socialist.

The Jungle Was Written as a Cry for Social Justice

Upton Sinclair

Upton Sinclair was the author of over ninety books.

At the age of twenty six, Sinclair arrived in Chicago to begin research for The Jungle. *He had already learned to hate poverty, and he championed socialism as a political force that could improve poor workers' living conditions. Happening upon a Lithuanian wedding one day, he found the material and the family that would serve as the focus for his first chapter and propel the novel. Because no publisher would print the novel without changes, he self-published* The Jungle *to worldwide acclaim. Its truth was challenged on several occasions, but independent researchers confirmed almost all of what he wrote.* The Jungle *has since moved many to take up social service, and it was the author's ardent wish that future readers would also be moved to serve others.*

On the twentieth of September, 1904, which happened to be a young writer's twenty-sixth birthday, he arrived in Chicago and put up in a small room of the Stockyards Hotel. He presented a letter of introduction to the University Settlement in the Stockyards district, then presided over by a wise and kindly lady named Mary MacDowell. He arranged to have his meals there for a modest sum, and spent the next seven weeks observing the life of the people in "Back of the Yards." He made the discovery that he could go anywhere in the immense packing plants by the simple device of wearing old clothes—he possessed no others—and carrying a workman's dinner-pail. In the evenings he sat in the workers' homes, asking questions and filling notebooks with what they told him.

Upton Sinclair, "Introduction," *The Jungle*, New York: Viking, 1950, pp. vii–xi.

Researching *The Jungle*

Toward the end of his stay, walking on a Sunday afternoon through the unpaved streets of this vast depressing slum, he saw a bridal couple alight from a hack [taxicab] and enter the rear room of a beer saloon. Other persons followed, and the writer joined them. No one appeared to have any objection to his presence, so he sat on a bench by the wall and watched a Lithuanian wedding supper and dance. Several who spoke English explained to him what was going on, and gradually he realized that this was the family he needed for his story. From four o'clock until nearly midnight he sat, making note of every detail and composing in his mind the opening chapter of a novel. By ten years of practice he had learned to go over a scene and fix it verbatim in his mind. This opening chapter was not put on paper until the following Christmas, but it varied little from the mentally recorded version.

The author had come from "the South," a part of the country impoverished by the Civil War. He had learned to hate poverty, and the limitations it put on his desire for learning, as well as its crushing effect on the dignity of men and women. He had discovered the Socialist party and ardently championed its program as the way to end poverty everywhere on earth. Now here it was in its ugliest aspects, the worst of which was the ignorance of its victims themselves. With the exception of a very small minority, they had no idea that they had the right to a better way of life. It was moral, spiritual, and physical degradation, a "jungle" in which humans lived barely above the level of animals.

The speech which concludes this novel reproduces one which the young writer himself delivered at a mass meeting in Chicago just before leaving for his home. It was the day on which Theodore Roosevelt was re-elected to the presidency; the speech was delivered in support of an unsuccessful [Socialist] candidate named Eugene V. Debs. If you get so far as the closing words of the speech you will see that the young author was far too optimistic. Chicago is still not "ours"; Chicago still belongs to the great vested interests. The dreadful sequence of world wars and counterrevolutions was mercifully veiled from the foresight of a young idealist.

Writing *The Jungle*

The Jungle was written in a board cabin, eight feet by ten, set on a hillside north of Princeton, New Jersey. The cabin had been built in part by the writer's hands, as were the table and bookshelf it contained; it was painted black, because that happened to be the cheapest kind of paint obtainable. The physical and mental sufferings about which you read in the story were those not merely of the Stockyards workers, but of a youth who had supported himself through nine years of college and university study, and was determined to survive as a writer or not at all.

Through a winter, spring, and summer he worked on the story, sometimes blinded by his own tears. It began appearing serially in the *Appeal to Reason*, a Socialist weekly which had a circulation of close to half a million, and the reaction was immediate. [Novelist] David Graham Phillips wrote: "I am reading *The Jungle*, and I should be afraid to trust myself to tell you how it affects me. It is so simple, so true, so tragic, and so human. I have a feeling that you yourself will be dazed some day by the excitement about it." The book was completed in September and offered to the author's last publishers, the Macmillan Company. The late George P. Brett said that he would publish it if some of the painful details were cut out. This was refused; and when four other publishers declined the book, the writer became impatient and invited the readers of the *Appeal to Reason* to make possible the publication by ordering copies and paying in advance.

An Overnight Sensation

[American novelist] Jack London wrote a broadside:

> Here it is at last! The book we have been waiting for these many years! The *Uncle Tom's Cabin* of wage slavery! Comrade Sinclair's book, *The Jungle!* And what *Uncle Tom's Cabin* did for black slaves, *The Jungle* has a large chance to do for the white slaves of today. . . .

> It is alive and warm. It is brutal with life. It is written of sweat and blood, and groans and tears. It depicts, not what man ought to be, but what man is compelled to be in this, our world, in the Twentieth Century. . . .

> All you have to do is to give this book a start. Once it gets its start, it will run away from you. The printers will be worked to death getting out larger and larger editions. It will go out by the hundreds of thousands. It will be read by every workingman. It will open countless ears that have been deaf to Socialism. It will plough the soil for the seed of our propaganda. It will make thousands of converts to our cause. Comrades, it is up to you!

The orders poured in—twelve thousand in all—and the book was put into type. At this point Doubleday, Page and Co. offered to publish the book, provided they could be satisfied as to its truth. They consulted a "friend" in Chicago, James Keeley, editor of the *Tribune*, who sent them what he said was "an impartial report" by his "best reporter," declaring that about everything in the book was false; it later turned out that the report had been composed by the publicity man of [the meatpacking moguls] the Armours. That was the beginning of a long series of attacks upon the book and its author, all of which have been narrated in *The Brass Check*, and which need not be repeated in this place. Suffice it to say that the publishers sent their lawyer to investigate, and he justified the work.

The Jungle appeared and became a sensation overnight, not merely in the United States, but in other countries. President [Theodore] Roosevelt sent for me, heard my story, and turned me over to two commissioners whom he ordered to make an investigation of Stockyards conditions. This was supposed to be secret, and I said not a word, but the packers knew all about it in a few hours and started their cleanup. Even so, the commission, after several weeks on the ground, turned in a report which sustained the book's charges. The commissioners told me that the only point on which they could get no proof was my statement that men had fallen into the lard vats and gone out to the world as pure leaf lard. Naturally this was a hard matter to prove, since in each case the families had been paid off and shipped to other parts of the world.

Success and Failure

Meantime *The Jungle* had become a best seller, and remained that for about six months. It was published in England, where it had the same success; the Hon. Winston Spencer Churchill wrote a two-part review of it. A German translation appeared quickly; it was probably the only book ever promoted by both Socialists and Junkers—the latter being the great landowners of Prussia, who were doing their best to obtain a tariff on imported meat. To date *The Jungle* has been translated into twenty-seven languages. It led to the quick passage of new meat-inspection laws, and this was some satisfaction to me, but was not my main interest. I wrote at the time that "I aimed at the public's heart and by accident I hit it in the stomach." This, I believe, has been the most widely quoted remark of my lifetime.

Forty years have passed, and the workers throughout America have fought a bitter war for a share of control over their own destinies. The workers of the Stockyards district have shared in this struggle and its benefits; they now have the Wagner Act, and a strong union to speak for them. Also there has started in "Back of the Yards" a movement for democratic action which you may read about in [labor organizer] Saul Alinsky's recent book, *Reveille for Radicals*. The labor of slaughtering animals is still hard and often dangerous; it is ill-paid and uncertain, as all labor must be so long as it is carried on under the profit system; but it is not so bad as it was forty years ago, and that much comfort can be offered to present-day readers of *The Jungle*.

Much Left to Learn—and Do

One of the pleasures which a twenty-six-year-old author enjoyed in Chicago was being invited to Hull House and sitting next to [American social reformer] Jane Addams at dinner. In the course of this occasion the ardent young Socialist delivered speeches such as you will find near the end of this book. He was told later that the saintly Jane had remarked to one of her associates, "That young man has a great deal to learn." Ten or twelve years later he met this high-hearted lady again, and reminded her of the remark. We agreed upon the statement that we had both had a great deal to learn, and that we had learned some of it and hoped to learn more. Man-made calamities have taught the author of *The Jungle* that he had placed far too high an estimate upon the intelligence of the human race, and its moral qualities. But he sees democracy spreading, both in industry and politics, and he still hopes to witness its victory, at least in his native land. The cry for social justice which echoes from these pages has been heard around the world, and leaders of the people's cause, both here and in other lands, have acknowledged that their first impulse toward social service came from [reading *The Jungle*]. May it be so with you!

Social Issues
in Literature

CHAPTER 2

The Jungle and Workers' Rights

The Jungle Depicted the Plight of Immigrant Workers

Jon A. Yoder

Jon A. Yoder served as associate dean at Idaho State University. He is the author of Decades of Decay: Upton Sinclair and American Liberalism After World War II.

Lured by the promise of good jobs and a better life, over a million and a half Russians immigrated to the United States in the first years of the twentieth century. But a strong work ethic, such as Jurgis Rudkus possessed, was not a guarantee of success. Conversely, for Sinclair, the capitalist system insured that only the unscrupulous man, willing to trade his morality for profits, would succeed in the American jungle. Sinclair proposed a solution in the form of democratic socialism, which would create a moral value system that could propel workers to success. But The Jungle *failed to stir Americans to political action. Instead, Sinclair felt, people focused narrowly on meat inspection instead of workers' rights.*

> Give me your tired, your poor, Your huddled masses yearning to breathe free, The wretched refuse of your teeming shore. Send these, the homeless, tempest-tost to me, I lift my lamp beside the golden door. —Emma Lazarus

When the Statue of Liberty was dedicated in 1886, the poetic sentiments carved on its pedestal had already achieved the status of national mystique. But the response to the invitation went beyond the imaginations of the Founding Fathers who had identified America as a land offering liberty and justice for all. During the first ten years of [the twentieth] century, 8,795,386 immigrants entered the United States. Although 8,135,016 of the people came from Europe, less than a half million were from Great Britain, whereas the number included more than two million Italians and another two million from Austria and Hungary. Certainly the Pilgrims, despite seeing themselves as models to be emulated, would never have predicted that within a single decade 1,597,306 Russians would follow their example in choosing this New World.

The Immigrant Experience

Since he wanted to give a current report on the state of the American experiment, Sinclair's creation of a Lithuanian immigrant family was quite appropriate. For significant Russian immigration (including Lithuanians) was a recent phenomenon. In 1880 only five thousand Russians [immigrated] to the United States. But this number increased steadily until 1907, one year after *The Jungle* was published, when more than a quarter of a million Russians bet their lives that America was their promised land.

If these were new sorts of immigrants, they were coming for traditional economic and religious reasons. And Sinclair, who never separated his economic condition from his spiritual or psychological state, was increasingly convinced that without socialism America could offer these new believers in the American Dream only a nightmarish existence. . . .

Working Harder

Throughout the first part of the book, Jurgis's response to increasing trouble is the one endorsed by Benjamin Franklin. When he finds that many of his wedding guests, especially the young ones, are abusing a time-honored custom by not contributing toward the costs of the affair he says, "I will work harder." When Ona [his wife] panics at his suggestion that she take a day's honeymoon away from work "he answers her again: 'Leave it to me; leave it to me. I will earn more money—I will work harder.'"

The immigrants, as Sinclair describes them, are faced with the difficult task of retaining desirable aspects of an old way of life—their music, their religion, their concept of family—within a new setting that affords, supposedly, the chance to succeed economically via personal efforts. According to scholars such as Oscar Handlin, this effort was doomed to fail from the time they got on board the boat in Europe: "The qualities that were desirable in the good peasant were not those conducive to success in the transition. Neighborliness, obedience, respect, and status were valueless among the masses that struggled for space on the way."

Not only do old ways fall victim to new conditions in Sinclair's novel, but the promise of equal economic opportunity for which these old values were sacrificed turns out to be fraudulent. Again Handlin supports Sinclair's earlier analysis: "It was characteristic that, about then [1900], for every hundred dollars earned by native wage earners, the Italian-born earned eighty-four, the Hungarians sixty-eight, and the other Europeans fifty-four."

The Law of the Jungle

Sinclair's title indicates that American society, in his analysis, had returned to the law of the jungle, where might makes right in a brutal survival of the fittest. But Sinclair was in no way one of those theorists who sought to apply the biological insights of [evolution theorist Charles] Darwin to the realm of social relationships. [Historian] John Higham has observed that "in their eagerness to convert social values into biological facts, Darwinian optimists unblinkingly read 'the fittest' to mean 'the best.'"

Sinclair directly opposed this. Rather than praising competition as a healthy and natural process—with cream always rising to the top—Sinclair accepted the contradictory value of cooperation. Competition, the socially inadequate law of the jungle, turns men into brutes in his novel:

> Every day the police net would drag hundreds of them off
> the streets, and in the Detention Hospital you might see

them, herded together in a miniature inferno, with hideous, beastly faces, bloated and leprous with disease, laughing, shouting, screaming in all stages of drunkenness, barking like dogs, gibbering like apes, raving and tearing themselves in delirium.

Those who survived the dehumanizing competition inherent in capitalism were likely to be the least fit morally. Later, in *The Goslings*, Sinclair would refer to Yale's professor of political economy, William Graham Sumner (a leading Social Darwinist), as "a prime minister in the empire of plutocratic education." And what Sumner called an objective analysis of the way society had to operate was called by Sinclair the deification of the most brutish sort of selfishness, "covered by the mantle of science." In short, the classic Social Darwinist statement of John D. Rockefeller represents quite precisely those ideas that Sinclair felt were antithetical to the American Dream:

The growth of a large business is merely a survival of the fittest. . . . The American Beauty rose can be produced in the splendor and fragrance which bring cheer to its beholder only by sacrificing the early buds which grow up around it. This is not an evil tendency in business. It is merely the working-out of a law of nature and a law of God.

In Sinclair's book, his version of reality, Jurgis cannot succeed financially without exchanging his high morality and willingness to work for a cynical acceptance of the need to lie, cheat, steal, and exploit others. . . .

The Socialist Answer

Sinclair's novel is remembered, and rightly so, for its graphic descriptions of working conditions in Packing-town. But only about half of the book is concerned with the meat-packing industry, and even this half is used as a vehicle for Sinclair's larger message. What had happened to the spirit of America?

What devil had tempted the American mind to substitute cash for value, thus allowing this intended Garden of Eden to go to seed—nourished by the heat of industrialization into a jungle of greed and grease and despair?

For Sinclair, bringing democracy to industry represented an answer to both economic and spiritual questions. He was not the first American to come to this conclusion. Earlier socialists, such as Edward Bellamy, had seen history as a working out of the gradual advance of the democratic principle. The Protestant Reformation had acknowledged all men as equal in status before God. The American and French Revolutions had introduced political equality. Now it was necessary to add economic equality in order to allow men their natural right to a humane and fulfilling existence.

Sinclair (who believed this) was a muckraker determined to expose the inhumanity of capitalism so that Americans could opt for an economic system more closely aligned with their accepted ideals. Not all muckrakers had such extensive ideological motivations. According to [noted historian] Richard Hofstadter, most

> outstanding figures of the muckrake era were simply writers or reporters working on commission and eager to do well what was asked of them. A few, among them Upton Sinclair and Gustavus Myers, were animated by a deep-going dislike of the capitalist order, but most of them were hired into muckraking or directed toward it on the initiative of sales-conscious editors or publishers.

As Hofstadter demonstrates, "what was new in muckraking in the Progressive era was neither its ideas nor its existence, but its reach—its nationwide character and its capacity to draw nationwide attention. . . ." So there was an element of fad in the success of Sinclair's novel. But since his goal was to upset an irrational economic system, he was scarcely satisfied by causing a nation to regurgitate. In *Cosmopolitan Magazine* (October 1906) Sinclair wrote:

Perhaps you will be surprised to be told that I failed in my purpose, when you know of all the uproar that "The Jungle" has been creating. But then that uproar is all accidental and was due to an entirely different cause. I wished to frighten the country by a picture of what its industrial masters were doing to their victims; entirely by chance I had stumbled on another discovery—what they were doing to the meat-supply of the civilized world. In other words, I aimed at the public's heart, and by accident I hit it in the stomach.

The Jungle as a Failure

To treat it fairly then, *The Jungle* must be considered from two points of view. Historically, it provided the impetus for useful legislation. Few writers accomplish this, and it should be remembered that Sinclair's goal was to affect the lives of his readers. For an understanding of why Sinclair considered it a failure, however, the novel must be evaluated in terms of his larger purpose—converting a populace to democratic socialism. . . .

It should be remembered that Sinclair wanted his writing to be very personal. *The Jungle*, in his opinion, was unlike the work of his contemporary producers of realistic literature because, as he wrote in *Cosmopolitan Magazine*, it was "written from the inside . . . the result of an attempt to combine the best of two widely different schools; to put the content of [English poet Percy Bysshe] Shelley into the form of [French novelist Émile] Zola." And Sinclair, personally, cared little about meat, since he rarely ate it.

But he did care deeply about what the meat industry typified and represented—the apparent failure on the part of American society to live up to established American ideals. The fact that his reading public responded to what he described as a symptom indicates his failure to communicate the more important concern about the basic illness.

Several explanations are supportable. Literature becomes impressive and memorable as it reduces abstract concepts to

Immigrants journey on the S.S. Patricia *from Hamburg, Germany, to New York City in 1906. Millions immigrated to the United States in the late nineteenth and early twentieth century looking for a better life. Sinclair felt many were being shamefully exploited after their arrival.* Edwin Levick/FPG/Getty Images.

concrete examples. It is easier to remember that children's fingers, cows' fetuses, and rat dung are the unlisted ingredients in deviled ham than that workers are oppressed, by definition, in a capitalist economy. Few readers, no matter how sympathetic, have found Sinclair's later chapters on socialist solutions to be as gripping as his preceding presentation of free enterprise at work. Through Jurgis, the reader learns about the advantages and imminence of socialism. But the speeches are tacked onto a plot that stops moving when Jurgis sits down to listen.

Sinclair, agreeing that the conclusion is weak, posits another explanation—one that fits in perfectly with his analysis of the intertwining of economic and spiritual concerns. He was too *poor* to turn his socialistic sermons into a more effective ending of *The Jungle*. In his *Autobiography* he writes: "The last chapters were not up to standard, because both my health and my money were gone, and a second trip to Chicago, which I had hoped to make, was out of the question."

In 1909 Sinclair again had reason to comment on the pernicious effect of money upon his career:

> Suffice it to say that never have I been able to write a single thing as I would have liked to write it, because of money. Either I was dead broke and had to rush it; or I knew that if I had my way, the public would not read it and the publishers would not accept it. Think of my having to ruin *The Jungle* with an ending so pitifully inadequate, because we were actually without money for food.

But even if philosophic solutions are harder to dramatize than scandalous situations, and even if Sinclair's efforts to make those solutions come to literary life were impeded by financial concerns, the public's positive response to Sinclair's described symptom (meat-packing conditions) while ignoring his deeper diagnosis (capitalistic greed), probably has more to do with audience than with author. If the story is read as exposing a scandal, a law can be passed, inspectors can be appointed to enforce that law, and we the people can receive a sense of continuing progress. This is far more palatable than reading the story as an indictment of one's entire way of life. To miss the basic point of any Sinclair writing requires strong motivation on the part of the reader. To look at what Sinclair was trying to teach is to discover what Americans were determined not to learn about themselves.

Beneath the rhetoric of a new society based on equality and brotherhood, America had built its experiment on tried and tested foundations of competition and greed. As indicated above, Jurgis personifies the willingness to accept individual responsibility for his own situation. He sets out across an ocean to solve his own problems through his own honest efforts; he wants to work. But by the turn of the century this point of view had become a demonstration of naiveté rather than of healthy optimism. Jurgis's co-laborers had already discovered that the game was rigged to allow only a few winners. So their response is the complete negation of the American Dream; they hate to work.

> They hated the bosses and they hated the owners; they hated the whole place, the whole neighborhood—even the whole city, with an all-inclusive hatred, bitter and fierce. Women and little children would fall to cursing about it; it was rotten, rotten as hell—everything was rotten.

Capitalism Rewards Immoral Behavior

For Sinclair, this undesirable result was built into the very theory of competitive capitalism:

> Here was Durham's, for instance, owned by a man who was trying to make as much money out of it as he could, and did not care in the least how he did it, and underneath him, ranged in ranks and grades like an army, were managers and superintendents and foremen, each one driving the man next below him and trying to squeeze out of him as much work as possible.

Men are not essentially evil, but within capitalism immoral behavior is systematically rewarded. Continuing his authorial comment in *The Jungle*, Sinclair contended:

> You could lay that down for a rule—if you met a man who was rising in Packingtown, you met a knave. . . . The man who told tales and spied upon his fellows would rise; but the man who minded his own business and did his work— why, they would "speed him up" till they had worn him out, and then they would throw him into the gutter.

Consequently, good men turn vicious in order to survive. Jurgis, who tries desperately to retain traditional values, yields to the stronger forces of inhumanity at the death of his son, "tearing up all the flowers from the garden of his soul, and setting his heel upon them." But Jurgis's creator retains those ideals, and he is in charge of the direction of the book. In his expression of very traditional American optimism, Sinclair believes that democracy will come to American industry because right eventually triumphs:

> Those who lost in the struggle were generally exterminated; but now and then they had been known to save themselves by combination—which was a new and higher kind of strength. It was so that the gregarious animals had overcome the predaceous; it was so, in human history, that the people had mastered the kings. The workers were simply the citizens of industry, and the Socialist movement was the expression of their will to survive.

The Happy Ending

Sinclair's happy ending, the conversion of Jurgis to a rational method of social organization, is made complete and personal via a charge of emotional energy:

> The voice of Labor, despised and outraged; a mighty giant, lying prostrate—mountainous, colossal, but blinded, bound, and ignorant of his strength. And now a dream of resistance haunts him, hope battling with fear; until suddenly he stirs, and a fetter snaps—and a thrill shoots through him, to the farthest ends of his huge body, and in a flash the dream becomes an act!. . . He springs to his feet, he shouts in his newborn exultation—

Nothing could be more traditionally American than the belief that this happy ending was inevitable since God was counted on the good side of the struggle. Socialism, for Sinclair, "was the new religion of humanity—or you might say it was the fulfillment of the old religion, since it implied but the literal application of all the teachings of Christ." Filtering [American revolutionary] Tom Paine through [American religionist] Jonathan Edwards, Sinclair preaches about the redemption of "a man who was the world's first revolutionist, the true founder of the Socialist movement. . . . Who denounced in unmeasured terms the exploiters of his own time. . . . This union carpenter! This agitator, lawbreaker, firebrand, anarchist!"

Workers Could Have Had It All

Answering the objection of those who do not believe in democratic socialism, Sinclair guaranteed the achievement of American equality through a rational distribution of wealth *without* totalitarian thought control:

> There was only one earth, and the quantity of material things was limited. Of intellectual and moral things, on the other hand, there was no limit, and one could have more without another's having less; hence "Communism in material production, anarchism in intellectual," was the formula of modern proletarian thought.

Sinclair's answer to the immigrants' problem applies the old solution, democracy, to the new conditions, industrialization and the emergence of mass man. Instead of the pathetic marriage of old immigrant values and new economic frustrations, Sinclair's solution insures that the survival of the fittest will also mean the perpetuation of the best. For example, Jurgis gets his first job as a socialist because a socialist employer has fired a man for drinking too much. The implication is clear; while the capitalist system drives a man to drink, if one drinks under socialism one *earns* dismissal.

The American people could have had all this, in Sinclair's opinion, simply by voting for their own interests. And they settled for federal meat inspection.

The Jungle Was Designed to Bolster the Labor Movement

Anthony Arthur

Anthony Arthur has taught at California State University–Northridge. He is the author of the book Literary Feuds: A Century of Celebrated Quarrels—from Mark Twain to Tom Wolfe.

Legend has it that even before doing the research for The Jungle, *Upton Sinclair announced that he was out to do nothing less than write the* Uncle Tom's Cabin *of the labor movement. In* Uncle Tom's Cabin, *Harriet Beecher Stowe had written a searing condemnation of slavery, and Sinclair was out to do the same for the working poor. But since no one was forcing workers to slave in the stockyards against their will, Sinclair did not have the same type of evil to attack. Sinclair, in fact, admired the systemic efficiency and machinery of the stockyards. What he disagreed with was the corporate greed that distorted the industrial system into one that destroyed even the strongest of individual workers. Thus, like Stowe, Sinclair produced a powerful, if flawed, attack on a corrupt system.* The Jungle *derives its force from powerfully narrated, horrific scenes that combine to indict the meatpacking industry.*

Ernest Poole, writing in 1940, vividly recalled Sinclair's appearance in the lobby of the Transit House upon his arrival in Chicago. A huge, rambling hotel next to the Union Stockyards, the Transit House was surrounded by porches and—in 1904—hitching posts. It was always jammed with cowboys, ranchers, and cattle dealers. It had also been the central meeting place for the stockyard workers' strike committee, to which Poole had offered his services. A favorite hangout for newspapermen and for writers looking for local color, the Transit House was the first place an inquisitive reporter new to town would visit. Poole was thus amused but not surprised when "in breezed a lad in a wide-breemed hat, with loose-flowing tie and a wonderful warm expansive smile. 'Hello! I'm Upton Sinclair!' he said. 'And I've come here to write the *Uncle Tom's Cabin* of the Labor Movement!'"

The Jungle vs. *Uncle Tom's Cabin*

Poole's memory of Sinclair's comment about Harriet Beecher Stowe's stirring novel sounds slightly apocryphal, echoing as it does what would come to be [American novelist] Jack London's later plug for *The Jungle*. But there is no doubt that Sinclair, fresh from an arduous year of work on [his Civil War novel] *Manassas*, had *Uncle Tom's Cabin* in mind when he arrived in Chicago. In *Manassas* he had linked Stowe's novel with two of his other favorites, [English writer John Bunyan's] *Pilgrim's Progress* and [English writer Daniel Defoe's] *Robinson Crusoe*, as great books "which make their way into the world of literature from below, and are classics before the *literati* have discovered them." It was still "the fashion" to denigrate *Uncle Tom's Cabin*, Sinclair wrote, "as having historical rather than literary interest." He admitted that as a work of literary art it was less than perfect—"its skeleton sticks through its every joint"—"but he who can read a hundred pages of it, for the first or the twentieth time, with dry eyes, is not an enviable person." *Uncle Tom's Cabin* remained, despite its imperfections, "the most unquestionable piece of inspiration in American fiction."

It certainly inspired Sinclair. He also envied what he considered Stowe's easier task, for she had the murderous Simon Legree [the villain in *Uncle Tom's Cabin*] to lash slaves and hound them across ice floes. The plight Sinclair wanted to describe seemed dull by comparison, and he was uncertain how to deal with it: "Who can thrill the reader with the tale of a man-hunt in which the hunted is a lousy and ignorant foreigner, and the hunters are the germs of consumption, diphtheria and typhoid? Who can make a romance out of the story of a man whose one life adventure is the scratching of a finger by an infected butcher knife, with a pine box and a pauper's grave as the denouement?"

Another problem for Sinclair was that slavery in pre–Civil War America had been a tangible reality, inflicted on black people who had often been dragged from their native villages, and who were routinely beaten, sometimes even killed when they protested or tried to escape. "Wage slavery" in the twentieth century was not a literal fact but a metaphor; no workers were chained to their jobs or shot for trying to quit. Moreover, as Sinclair noted, most of the workers in Chicago were foreigners who, rather than being kidnapped, had chosen to come here. The plight of workers in general might stir sympathy, even indignation, but their protests often came in the form of strikes that inconvenienced and antagonized the public—unlike the pre–Civil War uprisings by black slaves, which were far away and quickly crushed. The hard fact was that the largely middle-class Americans, mostly women, who bought and read books in the early 1900s were not likely to demand the end of "wage slavery." Workers' problems for these readers were mostly distant and theoretical concerns, no matter how vividly described.

The Stockyard Setting

Food, however, was an immediate and practical matter. Everyone had to eat; most people ate meat; and the meatpacking industry had been the subject of intense scrutiny for a decade. Sinclair made a calculated decision to use Chicago's slaughterhouses as the *setting* for his book because doing so would broaden his base of readers and appeal to their self-interest. His true *subject*, however, was to be the working conditions that he thought approximated slavery. His argument would be that the capitalistic system behind such conditions should give way to socialism. He had virtually no interest in persuading readers that their meat was rotten except as a means of dramatizing the sad conditions of the workers who prepared it for them. People could always choose not to eat meat. Workers couldn't choose not to work if they wanted to live.

The dramatic setting of the stockyards and the universal appeal of food as a subject still did not guarantee that Sinclair would be able to write the bestseller he had in mind. Most of the public believed that the meatpacking industry was a tribute to American technology and a boon to consumers, not a threat to its health. Following the Civil War and the completion of the nation's road network, a few aggressive innovators—P.D. Armour and Augustus Swift among them—built slaughterhouses near railroad terminals in major cities like Chicago. They also bought controlling interests in the stockyards where the animals were penned until they were killed. Local small-scale slaughterhouses scattered around the country could not compete with the big companies and their modern methods of manufacture, which depended on speed, size, and efficiency. By the end of the century, the livestock industry had become the nation's largest—even larger than mining or steel—and by the early 1900s it was becoming a force in the world market. Its greatest figure, Philip Danforth Armour, was lauded as "a sandy-haired, red-whiskered demigod of stock-yards mythology" by one contemporary, and generously profiled in a long interview with [writer] Theodore Dreiser as a "plain merchant" modest and courteous, who recoiled at the notion that he was "the Hercules of American industry.". . .

Sinclair agreed with [American novelist] Frank Norris that a novel could be as effective as a sermon in changing people's attitudes, and with [English poet Percy Bysshe] Shelley's claim that writers should lead the way to social change as the "legislators of mankind." But his own choice of imagery as he approached his task in Chicago was distinctly martial. He had to get inside the "fortress of oppression" without the enemy watching him: "How to breach those walls, or to scale them, was a military problem." He admitted later that he probably did not overwhelm his new comrades as a warrior. He had just turned twenty-six, still so dewy-cheeked that he could go for several days without shaving. He was "young and ascetic-looking," suffering so often from nervous tension, headaches, and indigestion that "my cheeks are hollow and my skin is white and my eyes have a hectic shine." He knew that to the experienced social workers and tough labor organizers he met in Chicago he seemed to be "a sort of 'guy,'" easily "pigeon-holed with long-haired violinists from abroad, and painters with fancy-colored vests, and women suffragists with short hair, and religious prophets in purple robes." He was a bumptious "young poet" who "believed that he had 'genius,' and kept making a noise about it."

But Sinclair was warmly received by capable men and women who were willing to take their new recruit in hand. Several were writers who had already done much of his legwork for him. Ernest Poole, his welcomer at the Transit House, graduated from Princeton in 1902, just a year before Sinclair moved there. An unusual Princetonian, at least from Sinclair's point of view, Poole had worked for a year at a New York settlement house, then moved to Chicago and become an unpaid publicity agent for the meatpackers union. He wrote an article about the stockyards strike for *The Independent* in July 1904, which Sinclair had read while preparing his own piece for the *Appeal*.

Poole's follow-up piece in August also caught Sinclair's eye. It was supposedly an autobiography, as told to Poole, of a Lithuanian immigrant stockyard worker named Antanas Kaztauskis. Disappointed in the failure of the American dream, Kaztauskis complained most bitterly about his experiences working in the stockyards. He also described being cheated by real estate agents (themselves immigrants) who persuaded him to buy a worthless house on a usurious installment plan. Theodore Roosevelt, always an avid reader, saw Poole's story and told an aide in Chicago to find out more about Kaztauskis. Poole explained that no such individual existed. He had written the story of thousands of men and given them one name, "Kaztauskis," as a representative symbol.

Elements of Poole's short narrative turn up in Sinclair's plot, including the cheating real estate agents. Another writer, Algie Simons, acted as Sinclair's "inside man," providing him with contacts that would help him pose as a worker. Simons was a socialist and sometime labor organizer who worked for the Bureau of Charities as its agent in the stockyards. He also served as a volunteer inspector for the Chicago Health Department. In 1899 Simons had written a pamphlet called "Packingtown," which contained many of the details and anecdotes that would make *The Jungle* so controversial. One described the death of a worker's child in a roadside pool of "slime," which Sinclair would use himself to strong effect in his novel. . . .

A Flawed but Powerful Novel

Like *Uncle Tom's Cabin*, *The Jungle* is hardly flawless. Some readers find their compassion for Jurgis and his family and friends giving way to incredulity at such an implausible accumulation of disasters. They grow numb, and avert their eyes from such horrors as the child who goes into convulsions and dies from eating smoked sausage, or the young boy who falls into a stupor after drinking beer and is eaten by rats. The "message" part of the novel also presents problems; Sinclair himself thought the second half of his book was too episodic and preachy, and he disliked the happy ending for Jurgis that he had felt compelled to provide: he had wanted to send him to jail for two years. But these weaknesses pale in comparison to Sinclair's great strengths in *The Jungle*: powerfully descriptive prose, a sense of truthful authority, and an inspiring moral fervor. . . .

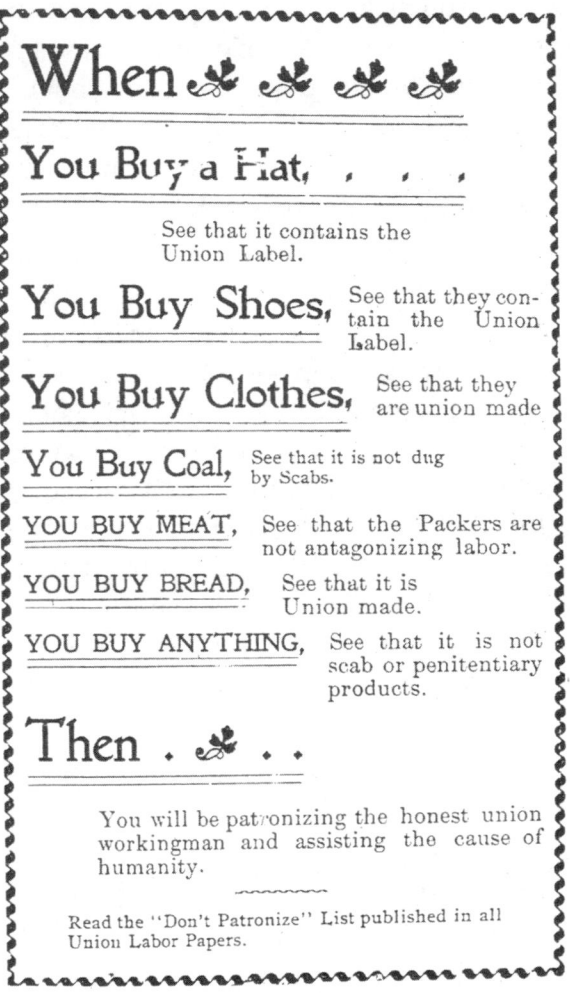

An 1895 poster calls on readers to buy union products and support organized labor. Sinclair hoped The Jungle *would increase support for the labor movement.* MPI/Getty Images.

The drama and color of Sinclair's artfully chosen details give his passage a kinetic force, a dynamic intensity paradoxically drawn from filth and decay. Similarly, what in Poole is just a "big smell" becomes for Sinclair's immigrants a "strange, pungent odor. . . . You could literally taste it, as well as smell it." Most writers would have stopped here, but Sinclair continues, endowing the disgusting odors with a strangely aesthetic appeal and his immigrants with qualities of sophisticated insight and curiosity that go beyond simple realism into symbolism: "you could take hold of it, almost, and examine it at your leisure. They were divided in their opinions about it. It was an elemental odor, raw and crude; it was rich, almost rancid, sensual, and strong. There were some who drank it in as if it were an intoxicant; there were others who put their handkerchiefs to their faces."

A Surreal Intensity

Sinclair also brings the slaughterhouse chimneys to malevolent life: "tall as the tallest of buildings, touching the very sky—and leaping from them half a dozen columns of smoke, thick, oily, and black as night. It might have come from the center of the world, this smoke, where the fires of the ages still smolder. . . . One stared, waiting to see it stop, but still the great streams rolled out. They spread in vast clouds overhead, writhing, curling; then, uniting in one giant river, they streamed away down the sky, stretching a black pall as far as the eye could reach."

Finally, Poole's vague reference to "the dumps" becomes in *The Jungle*, an explanation of how the workers' houses occupy old dump sites where the city's garbage still festers a few feet underground, resulting in "swarms of flies . . . blackening the air" and "a ghastly odor, of all the dead things of the universe."

Sinclair's descriptions often achieve a surreal intensity: Jurgis carefully watches the doomed hogs, who must approach "a great iron wheel, about twenty feet in circumference," studded with large iron rings. A "great burly Negro, bare-armed and bare-chested," tends the wheel, turning it as two men seize a pig, attach a loop of chain to its rear, and secure the other end of the chain to a ring of the wheel. The wheel revolves, and the hog is "suddenly jerked off his feet and borne aloft," shrieking in pain and fear until its throat is slit and it vanishes "with a splash into a huge vat of boiling water." This is "pork-making by machinery, pork-making by applied mathematics." Sinclair's description here is worthy of his admirer [surrealist author] Franz Kafka, and is partly echoed, consciously or not, in Kafka's treatment of the ingenious killing machine in his story "In the Penal Colony."

In one of his more purple passages—which he later insisted, not very convincingly, he intended as satire—Sinclair allows Jurgis to speculate on the harmless victims of the machine: "they were so innocent, they came so very trustingly; and they were so very human in their protests. . . . And now was one to believe that there was nowhere a god of hogs, to whom this hog personality was precious, to whom these hog squeals and agonies had a meaning? Who would take this hog into his arms and comfort him, reward him for his work well done, and show him the meaning of his sacrifice? Perhaps some glimpse of all this was in the thoughts of our humble-minded Jurgis as he turned to go on with the rest of the party and muttered: '*Dieve*—but I'm glad I'm not a hog!'"

Graphic Realism

Sinclair's descriptions of the workers' lives and the conditions of their employment—his true subject in *The Jungle*—generally eschew symbolism in favor of graphic realism: "Of the butchers and floorsmen, the beefboners and trimmers, and all those who used knives, you could scarcely find a person who had the use of his thumb; time and time again the base of it had been slashed, till it was a mere lump of flesh against which the man pressed the knife to hold it." In another passage Sinclair describes how the men working on the unheated "killing-beds" in subzero winter weather would bury their frozen hands and feet within the steaming carcass of the steer they had just killed. Much of *The Jungle* is devoted to similar depictions of such uncomfortable and dangerous working conditions. Hardly less important, though less sensational, is the persistent exploitation of the workers by everyone they encounter: saloonkeepers, aldermen [city councilmen], the police, and their own countrymen.

By comparison, relatively few pages, perhaps thirty in all, describe the details of unhealthy procedures relating to meat products. Lurid and revolting, these were the passages that would make *The Jungle* so controversial and so successful— and that completely overshadowed the plight of the workers so earnestly depicted by Sinclair.

Ironically, most of the abuses that led to public concern for the safety of their meat products stemmed from the excess of two great virtues prized by American business enterprises: the avoidance of waste and the maximizing of efficiency. Meat-packing was a labor-intensive enterprise, highly competitive, with a slender margin of profit. Then as now, Americans paid far less for their food than Europeans, which accounts in part for their tolerance of peculiarities, and even of abuses, in its manufacture. In their efforts to avoid waste, and to increase profits, the packers used everything they could from slaughtered animals, including snouts, tails, horns, hooves, eyeballs, entrails, and skins: "everything but the squeal." In order to increase production and hold down costs, they developed, as an admiring biography of P. D. Armour noted in 1938, "the basic device of modern straight line production. . . . The 'assembly line' and 'belt' of the modern motor car, chemical, or electrical equipment plant are merely an adaptation of the 'chain' which came into packing-plants in 1865 or thereabouts."

Sinclair Admired Efficiency and Hard Work

Although he deplored the dehumanizing effects of working at repetitive, boring tasks, Sinclair had no quarrel with the ideal of efficiency, and he revered the idea of work itself. Unlike the followers of [English socialist poet] William Morris and others who wanted to retreat to some kind of imaginary preindustrial utopia, he was, he said, "a Socialist who believes in machinery." There was "no reason why machines should not make beautiful and substantial things," instead of ugly ones, other than the system that allows people to make profits from them. Sinclair's memorable phrase, "pork-making by applied mathematics," does not signal ironic disdain but admiration, just as Jurgis's pride at being "a sharer in all this activity, a cog in all this marvelous machine" is sincere.

Equally sincere, and admirable for Sinclair, is Jurgis's evident belief that hard work has its own inherent satisfaction, even shoveling steaming heaps of guts. He wants to work, to belong. It was not the system of industrial production or the killing of animals for food that Sinclair was attacking, or the fact that some people had to do unpleasant but necessary work. He was attacking what he regarded as the *distortion* of the industrial system, the warping of the machine, caused by the uncontrolled drive for profit.

For Sinclair, this distortion showed itself in four ways. First, the packers' use of diseased or condemned animal parts; second, their use of chemical additives; third, their indifference to workers' health and welfare, resulting in dangerous contamination of food products; and fourth, their resistance to state and federal regulations that would control these practices and attitudes. Sinclair wove his objections into a series of passages that would frequently be excerpted in newspaper stories about *The Jungle*. Each read like a short horror story. Combined, they amounted to an indictment. . . .

Sinclair Distorted Conditions in Packingtown

Louise Carroll Wade

Louise Carroll Wade has taught at the University of Oregon. She is the author of Graham Taylor: Pioneer for Social Justice, 1851–1938 *and* Chicago's Pride: The Stockyards, Packingtown, and Environs in the Nineteenth Century.

Upton Sinclair's portrait of immigrant life in turn-of-the-century Chicago is a fabrication and a distorted portrait of reality. In order to drive home his point, Sinclair exaggerates the ills of Packingtown life. From workers' wages to housing woes to neighborhood life to the influence of the church and saloons on immigrants, Sinclair's depictions are false. He continually makes life seem worse than it was for these newcomers to America and fails to depict accurately the positive attributes of Packingtown, such as home ownership and church life. Sinclair's depiction of politics is equally distorted, and he ignores the manner in which immigrant workers had an important role in Chicago elections.

If *The Jungle* misrepresents packers and packinghouse products, it is even more misleading about the workers and their community. In order to prove that they exist in an "inferno of exploitation," Sinclair lets bosses, realtors, merchants, politicians, priests, saloon keepers and the midwife cheat the Rudkus clan. Jurgis is "helpless as a wounded animal, the target of unseen enemies," his wife too child-like to cope, and stolid Elzbieta, the linchpin of the group, reminds him of "the angleworm, which goes on living though cut in half . . . she asked no questions about the justice of it, nor the worthwhileness of life in which destruction and death ran riot." Little wonder the

Louise Carroll Wade. "The Problem with Classroom Use of Upton Sinclair's *The Jungle*," *American Studies*, vol. 32, no. 2, fall 1991, pp. 79–101. Copyright © Mid-American Studies Association, 1991. Reproduced by permission of the publisher.

journal published by the packinghouse workers' union called the novel "greatly overdrawn" and objected to a plot in which the immigrants experience "only slavery, injustice and death."

Sinclair Distorted Workers' Wages

Sinclair wanted readers to believe that packinghouse workers were "rats in a trap," that prostitutes fared better than "decent" girls, and that "if you met a man who was rising . . . you met a knave." John R. Commons of the University of Wisconsin studied the Chicago packinghouse workers in 1904 and described the great variety of jobs commanding wages from 15 cents an hour for new unskilled hands to 50 cents an hour for the highly skilled "butcher aristocracy." He found that Irish and German newcomers in the 1880s had moved up, "accumulated money," and were fanning out into other jobs. Bohemians dominated the skilled ranks, while newly-arrived Slovaks and Lithuanians filled the lower positions. He did meet one Slovak who had been in Packingtown for ten years and "worked himself up to a 50-cent job." Another academic investigator, Carl William Thompson, studied the district in 1906 and came to similar conclusions. Even laborers were able to save part of their earnings, and "Slovak and Lithuanian girls working . . . at the low wage of five dollars a week also save a considerable fraction of their income." A recent study of Chicago's low-wage women workers who chose to live apart from family and relatives found that most managed to do so. Ernest Poole's protagonist advanced from five dollars per week in his first job to eleven dollars per week and said that was "very common. There are thousands of immigrants like me."

Adults in the Rudkus family eventually join the union but find it cannot protect their jobs and its venal leaders are part of the army of Chicago grafters. So Jurgis becomes a strikebreaker and helps destroy it. Commons, Thompson, Poole, Mary McDowell, labor statistician Ethelbert Stewart and more recently David Brody and James Barrett have much higher opinions of the union than does Sinclair. Chartered in 1897 by the American Federation of Labor to sign up packinghouse and market butchers, it made an important difference in Packingtown. Run by skilled men, it nonetheless was willing and able to organize unskilled, female and black workers. It wrested from the packers wage increases, shorter and steadier hours, and promotions based on seniority. Moreover, it was the only organization that brought together the various ethnic groups employed in Packingtown. In other words, packinghouse workers as viewed by contemporaries and recent scholars bear little resemblance to what Barrett calls Sinclair's "hopeless, animal-like creatures."

Sinclair Exaggerated Housing Woes

Most of them made wiser housing decisions than did the Rudkus family. Upon their arrival the Rudkus family crowds into a Lithuanian woman's "unthinkably filthy" flat. It is one of four flats in a two-story building, and according to Sinclair such structures usually had from six to fourteen people per room, "fifty to sixty to a flat." The next step for most immigrant families would have been their own four-room flat, renting for $9 a month. But Sinclair's group decides within one week to invest their combined savings in a supposedly new four-room house, "a long mile and a half" from the packing plants. Its basement and attic are unfinished so they cannot take boarders, and it will cost them $12 per month plus interest, insurance, real estate taxes and water, which they do not understand. Inexplicably they look at nothing else: "they did not know where any more were, and they did not know any way of finding out." "In short order they discover that their house is fifteen years old, infested with cockroaches, incredibly cold in winter, and unlucky. Every family that lived in it, someone was sure to get consumption." After Jurgis goes to jail, the others fall behind in the payments and lose the house, furnishings and down payment.

Knowledgeable contemporaries did not share Sinclair's grim assessment. Robert Hunter omitted the district from his study of substandard Chicago housing because "there is no large area . . . where the conditions seem to be uniformly bad." "Very few of the houses . . . are deficient in provisions for light and ventilation, and none of them seem to be overcrowded." He did fault some for inadequate drainage and filthy yards, but those "evils do not extend over a large area. They are, in their worst forms, extraordinary and not typical." After examining the residential area around the packinghouses, Adolphe Smith said the employees were "very fortunate to be able to live in what . . . is more like the country than a city boasting of nearly 2,000,000 inhabitants." The houses had "plenty of air space around them," were "not in bad condition," were "fairly clean," and "overcrowding . . . was not general." He thought the "unwholesomeness" of the packinghouses was "to a large extent counteracted by the healthy character of the workpeople's houses."

A Typical Neighborhood

Nor did observers agree with Sinclair about the degree of overcrowding. It was Hedger's opinion that the two-story, four-flat rental buildings sheltered "four families on the average," each with four adults and "some children thrown in for good measure"—a far cry from Sinclair's claim of fifty or sixty per flat. Ethelbert Stewart's unpublished 1905 survey of 284 Back of the Yards dwellings found some with boarders, some without, some clean, some dirty. Newcomers were more apt to have boarders than, say, the Polish family of five who after six years in Packingtown had its own "Well lighted, neat & clean, well furnished" four-room flat. In 1909 [educators and social activists] Sophonisba Breckinridge and Edith Abbott studied over six hundred "typical" frame houses in a ten block area that was predominantly Polish and Lithuanian. Though most of the houses were built before the city's 1903 housing ordinance, more than four-fifths met the new standards. And fewer than one-quarter of the people living in those structures were lodgers. Breckinridge and Abbott, like most middle-class Americans, disapproved of the immigrant practice of taking lodgers or boarders, but they understood that those families had lived in close quarters in their homelands and that the additional income helped them achieve their goal of home ownership. Thus the houses and the occupants, they said, were like immigrant working-class districts elsewhere in Chicago and in other cities; Back of the Yards was "a typical and not an exceptional neighborhood."

The Church and the Saloons

During his stay in Packingtown Sinclair found "no ray of sunshine in the lives of the people, save such as they were able to get out of drunkenness." Hence his Lithuanian characters steer clear of the church, join no ethnic organizations, and befriend only "near neighbors and shopmates." Since there were eight ethnic Catholic churches in the Stockyards district, half of them imposing in size, an observer would have to be blind and deaf to miss their significance. Charles Bushnell, author of a 1902 doctoral dissertation about the community, considered those churches and their many societies the "centers of social intercourse." Carl William Thompson noted that the various ethnic groups had "their own societies and clubs, and all belong to the same church." Although Poole's Lithuanian was not a regular church-goer, he belonged to the Lithuanian Concertina Club and another society which gave "two picnics in summer and two big balls in winter." "On Sundays we go on the trolley out into the country." Another observer said "principal thoroughfares" in every Chicago working-class district were "gay all summer with the banners announcing the picnic of one or another of these lodges." Churches and ethnic organizations were "social anchors" in the development of Back of the Yards in the late nineteenth century, and Robert

Slayton refers to the church as the "central institution" in his study of the community in the first half of the twentieth century.

Only in *The Jungle* are saloons so evil. Two Chicago investigators for the Committee of Fifty said those in working-class districts were "a part of the life of the people," "the workingman's club." Patrons read newspapers and played cards, exchanged views and secured employment information, cashed their pay checks, and had free lunches with their beer. In the saloons of the Hull House ward, E.C. Moore was unable to find "a riotous company intent upon reducing itself to intoxication." Drinking was not "the most important thing." Breckinridge and Abbott discovered that the 1,268 Polish and Lithuanian households in their study supported thirty drinking establishments, most of them at corner locations with other stores. The saloon keeper was "a person of influence, and the hall in the rear . . . a social center in which weddings and other festivities occur." In addition, John Kingsdale's "The 'Poor Man's Club,'" Perry Duis's authoritative study of saloons in Chicago and Boston, and Slayton's *Back of the Yards* cast fatal doubt on the accuracy of Sinclair's depiction.

A Farcical Treatment of Politics

Also misleading is Sinclair's farcical treatment of politics. Voters are dolts, elections are ritual jousts between "rival sets of grafters," and Jurgis sells his services to a "political lord" with "rat-like eyes," "a little dried-up Irishman, whose hands shook." Almost certainly the novelist saw [American author] Lincoln Steffens' "Chicago: Half Free and Fighting On" in the October 1903 issue of *McClure's* or [Steffens' book] *The Shame of the Cities* (1904). Yet there is no hint in *The Jungle* of the hotly contested aldermanic elections or Steffens' assertion that the Municipal Voters' League had "something to teach every city and town in the country." While Sinclair was writing—and wishing to make a second trip to Chicago—he could have followed the 1905 race for mayor. An outspoken Irish-American Democrat, Edward F. Dunne, won that election with the help of the Chicago Federation of Labor and immigrant workers, including those in the Stockyards district.

The Jungle's Truths Cannot Be Ignored

Winston Churchill

As prime minister, Winston Churchill led England during World War II and is one of the leading historical figures of the twentieth century. He is the author of more than forty books about history and society.

Upton Sinclair's The Jungle *is a powerful novel written by a man of great gifts bent on reforming abuses in contemporary society and replacing the current political administration with a socialist alternative. Sinclair does not shrink away from relating even the most horrific facts, and if even one small portion of his sordid tale of life in the meatpacking industry is true, then he has done society a great favor. Jurgis and his family suffer through abject misery at the hands of the Chicago Beef Trust. There are no easy answers to solving these widespread problems, but this book should lead the way in reforming society.*

When I promised to write a few notes on this book *The Jungle*, I had an object—I hoped to make it better known. In the weeks that have passed that object has disappeared. The book has become famous. It has arrested the eye of a warm-hearted autocrat; it has agitated the machinery of a State department; and having passed out of the sedate columns of the reviewer into leading articles and "latest intelligence," has disturbed in the Old World and the New the digestions, and perhaps the consciences, of mankind.

Bringing Down the "Beef Trust"

Mr. Upton Sinclair is one of that active band of reformers, comprising some men of very great gifts and some men of

Winston S. Churchill, "The Chicago Scandals," *The Great Republic: A History of America*, New York: Random House, 1999, pp. 259–269. Preface, additional text, and compilation copyright © 1999 by Winston S. Churchill. Maps copyright © 1999 by Anita Karl and Jim Kemp.Reproduced by permission of Random House, Inc. and Curtis Brown Ltd, London, on behalf of The Estate of Winston Churchill.

very great wealth, whose energies are now directed in the United States to no less a task than the destruction or bodily capture of the Democratic party and the installation in its place of a thorough and unshrinking Socialist organization. His book is a tract in a swelling political agitation, and it takes the form of an indictment of the huge meat-packing business on the shores of Lake Michigan popularly called the great "Beef Trust." Nothing can exceed the skill and determination with which the author has marshalled his arguments. He is one of those debaters who stand no nonsense from their facts. He finds a place for each—even for the most contrary—in ingenious sequences which steadily approach his goal. All conditions of life—social, moral, political, economic, commercial, climatic, bacteriological—are assembled [and] drilled into order ... One purpose and one purpose alone animates the mind of the commander, and inspires his army down to the humblest item which marches silently in the ranks—to make the great Beef Trust stink in the nostrils of the world, and so to contaminate the system upon which it has grown to strength. Here in the compass of a few hundred pages has been collected all that can be said against the canning industry, all that will damage it before its servants and expose it to its customers.

The "packers" are brought to the bar. The goods they sell, the materials they use, the city they dwell in, the wages they pay—every circumstance, great and small, of their business, together with its consequences, direct or remote—are subjected to a pitiless and malevolent scrutiny.

The worst has been told, and only the worst; it has been told in the most effective way; and the reader is confronted—nay, overwhelmed—by concatenations [series of] of filthy, tragic, detestable details, which reduce him, however combative or incredulous, to a kind of horror-struck docility.

Let me say at once that people have no right to hold their noses and shut their eyes. If these things are true, all honour to him who has the power and skill to fasten world-wide attention upon them. If they be only half true, a great public service has been rendered. If only one-tenth part be true, there would still, I fancy, be some debt owing by society to Mr. Upton Sinclair. And there is, unhappily, good reason to believe—scarcely, indeed, any reason to doubt—that a very considerable body of undeniable and easily ascertainable truth sustains the charges that are made. Mr. Upton Sinclair has done for the "packers" what Mr. Henry Lloyd did some years ago in *Wealth against Commonwealth* for the Standard Oil Trust. The mood and the motive of both books are the same; but in one respect Mr. Sinclair's method has a great advantage over his forerunner. *Wealth against Commonwealth* was a laborious compilation. *The Jungle* is a human tragedy.

A Tale of Simple, Industrious Folk

The thread on which all is strung is the gradual ruin, moral and physical, of a strong, brave, honest man. We are introduced abruptly to a family of Lithuanian peasants who have migrated to Chicago. The family is numerous. All relationships and all ages are included. There is Jurgis the hero, a mighty man, a Titan among workers. There is Ona, the girl to whom he is pledged, and for whose sake the great adventure of the ocean voyage has been made. There are her father and aunt, and his brother and his sister, Marija, and four or five small children of varying ages. All the grown-ups are thrifty, industrious, simple Lithuanian folk who, having massed their savings, have sailed for the United States, and after being fleeced by every official into whose clutches their journey has led them, have arrived at length at Chicago, asking nothing better than to work from dawn to dusk at an honest trade.

The characters are drawn with care and feeling. We get to know them all. We get to like them all. We become swiftly interested in their domestic economy. How much is left to them of their slender stock of money, what are their prospects of

*This child lost his arm in an accident while working in a box fac-
tory, circa 1909.* The Jungle *exposed how industry exploited workers
of all ages without regard for their welfare.* Lewis W. Hine/George
Eastman House/Getty Images.

employment, what wages are they bringing in each week, what
debts and expenses have they to meet, what perils are in their
path—all these petty, everyday matters are made real and important to us by a hundred pages of lively and elaborate art.
Once this has been accomplished, Mr. Upton Sinclair has the
reader very much at his mercy. He uses his advantage to the
full. The utter destruction of this whole family in circumstances of misery and horrid degradation is the plan on which

he proceeds, and which he carries out in an exquisite detail and with a ruthlessness of purpose which certainly leave nothing to be desired from an artistic point of view. . . .

No Easy Answer

The reader will not, I think, be satisfied with this conclusion. After all that has happened, after all that has been suffered, he will look for some more complete consolation. Not so Mr. Upton Sinclair. This shrewd delineator of character, this painstaking and careful exponent of detail, appears sincerely unconscious of our disappointment. Consolation?—have we not the Socialist orator? Regeneration?—is not Jurgis fully instructed? Salvation?—who can doubt the earnestness of his convictions? What more can anyone require? Let us rejoice that through all this filth and agony one heart at least has been saved from error. There is one man more in Chicago who may be trusted to vote straight for the Socialist ticket. Hurrah!

In writing thus I do not mean to carp at the really excellent and valuable piece of work which this terrible book contains. It pierces the thickest skull and the most leathery heart. It forces people who never think about the foundations of society to pause and wonder. It enables those who sometimes think to understand. The justification of that vast and intricate fabric of Factory Law, of Health Acts, of Workmen's Compensation, upon which Parliament is swiftly and laboriously building year by year and month by month, is made plain, so that a child may see it, so that a fool may see it, so that a knave may see it. But I must frankly say that if the conditions of society in Chicago are such as Mr. Upton Sinclair depicts, no mere economic revolution would in itself suffice to purify and ennoble. A National or Municipal Beef Trust, with the United States Treasury at its back, might indeed give more regular employment at higher wages to its servants, and might sell cleaner food to its customers—at a price. But if evil systems corrupt good men, it is no less true that base men will dishonour any system, and while no bond of duty more exacting than that of material recompense regulates the relations of man and man, while no motion more lofty than that of self-interest animates the exertions of every class, and no hope beyond the limits of this fleeting world lights the struggles of humanity, the most admirable systems will merely succeed in transferring, under different forms and pretexts, the burden of toil, misery, and injustice from one set of human shoulders to another.

It is possible that this remarkable book may come to be considered a factor in far-reaching events. The indignation of millions of Americans has been aroused. That is a fire which has more than once burnt with a consuming flame. There are in the Great Republic in plentiful abundance all the moral forces necessary to such a purging process. The issue between Capital and Labour is far more cleanly cut today in the United States than in other communities or in any other age. It may be that in the next few years we shall be furnished with Transatlantic answers to many of the outstanding questions of economics and sociology upon whose verge British political parties stand in perplexity and hesitation. And that is, after all, an additional reason why English readers should not shrink from the malodorous recesses of Mr. Upton Sinclair's *Jungle*.

Sinclair Was Disappointed by the Impact of *The Jungle*

Kevin Mattson

Kevin Mattson has taught at Ohio University. He has written regularly for the Nation, *the* American Prospect *and the* New York Times Book Review. *His books include* When America Was Great: The Fighting Faith of Postwar Liberalism *and* Democracy's Moment: Reforming the American Political System for the 21st Century.

In the years before he wrote The Jungle, *Sinclair became completely preoccupied by socialism, which he believed held the answer to improving conditions for workingmen and -women. This was a time when reform was a popular notion in America, and reform movements found their champion in President Theodore Roosevelt. After the publication of* The Jungle, *with its lurid vignettes of workers' abuse, Roosevelt contacted Sinclair and the two met at the White House. But Roosevelt's reforms, which centered on creating more sanitary meatpacking conditions, were not enough for Sinclair. He believed that only a complete transfer from a capitalist to a socialist system would cure America's ills. He kept badgering the president to do more, until Roosevelt had to remind him who was president and who was a mere muckraker.*

From 1904 to 1905, socialism overtook Upton Sinclair's consciousness. He could think of little else; this dream of a better world allowed him to escape the domestic hell of his marriage and the poverty of his Princeton [New Jersey] cabin. Socialism allowed him to direct his crusading spirit in another direction. Sinclair no longer wanted to be a romantic poet decrying the philistine book publishing world, nor did he want to be an underread author. He wanted to reach large numbers of Americans in order to grow the ranks of the Socialist Party and use his gift of publicity and writing for a cause. In 1905 he found his moment.

The Right Time for Reform

There were important changes underway in America at the time. On September 16, 1901, President William McKinley, the man who led the United States into the Spanish-American War, was shot by an anarchist. Suddenly, Theodore Roosevelt was propelled into the presidency. Roosevelt turned out to be a bold president who never forgot his predecessor's assassination. He wanted to prevent future chaos in the country, not by jailing every radical out there but by eliminating the causes of their most strident and politically poignant complaints. He passed social and political legislation that confronted the problems generated by industrialization, problems he believed allowed radical assassins to justify their actions against a recalcitrant system. He described his presidency as "a corrective to Socialism and an antidote to anarchy" and pledged himself to "conservative radicalism." He stood up to the businessmen who wanted to use their economic power for selfish political aims. When Roosevelt attacked the interests of J. P. Morgan, America's most powerful banker, Morgan messaged the White House to inquire. "If we have done something wrong," Morgan said, "send your man to my man and they can fix it up." Roosevelt's response was a resounding: "That can't be done." In a stance that, in many ways, epitomized the times, he drew a line in the sand between the White House and corporate influence, pursuing what he considered to be the public good. When coal-mining companies refused to negotiate with striking miners, Roosevelt threatened to nationalize the mines. When he learned that private loggers were devastating

America's forests, he pledged himself to conservation. His was an activist and reformist presidency.

Roosevelt's action from on high reflected growing concerns coming from below. He knew about the activism of settlement houses, where studies of child labor and other forms of exploitation were being conducted. In the case of the coal strike, Roosevelt noted labor unions organizing to provide an outlet for the anger of overworked and underpaid employees. He had also read work by a group of writers he called "muckrakers," who kept bringing up "the filth of the floor" so that everyone could see it. These journalists wrote stories about corruption, about how companies like Standard Oil, owned by John D. Rockefeller, destroyed competition in underhanded ways—by bribing railroads so that they would refuse to carry the goods of competitors or by threatening competitors directly with physical violence. These stories reached large numbers of middle-class readers in magazines like *McClure's*. Middle-class readers voted and expressed concern about the fate of the country, further energizing the work of politicians like Roosevelt to do something. Reform movements were gaining steam at this time, and it was in that atmosphere that Sinclair's *The Jungle* appeared. . . .

Chicago: The Perfect Setting

"I spent seven weeks in the stockyards district alone, living with the people, meeting with them in their homes, in the places where they worked, in their saloons and clubs." While compiling facts, Sinclair never dropped his prejudices. He followed in the footsteps of southern social critics who decried the industrializing society of the North. Southern writers during the antebellum period, like George Fitzhugh, for instance, delighted in telling northerners that they were no better than the South—"cannibals all!"—since wage work was more degrading than slavery. Sinclair himself believed that southern slaves had it better than wage earners. But he had taken the time to do research to justify his regional prejudices.

Chicago was the perfect city for Sinclair to set his novel, a place where all of America's new problems and progress were fiercely converging. To celebrate the four-hundredth anniversary of Columbus's voyage in 1893, the city erected a set of buildings named the White City and held an enormous exposition to celebrate industrial and moral progress in the country. It's now known that the work done to erect the White City was incredibly exploitative for its immigrant workers. Chicago had already had its fair share of strikes and labor conflicts, most famously the Haymarket Affair of 1886 and the Pullman strike a year after the White City went up. In 1904 meatpacking workers walked off the job, and this was the incident that prompted Sinclair's visit. Chicago had become a place of violence and strife—a perfect setting for a dramatic novel like *The Jungle*. Besides, Chicago had already provided background for realist novels, like Theodore Dreiser's *Sister Carrie* (1900), a shocking story about a young woman moving from a small Wisconsin farm to the industrial underbelly of Chicago and embarking on an affair with a married man. . . .

An Equal Opportunity Exploiter

If Chicago was the perfect city, the meatpacking industry was the perfect line of business for Sinclair to investigate. It was a quintessential trust that had centralized its economic power. Meatpacking demanded the sort of management systems central to modern business. As one economic historian explained, a beef trust robber baron like Gustavus Franklin Swift had to coordinate the "purchases of live animals, the activities of its large slaughtering and butchering plants in the Midwest, and the transport of its dressed beef" in order to "match the fluctuating demand in the cities where the meat was consumed." Swift and J. Ogden Armour could afford to invest in refrigerated train cars; those companies that couldn't simply died off. By 1899, according to Algie Simons, a socialist who helped Sinclair gather information for *The Jungle*, competition was officially dead in the meat industry. And with centralized economic power came centralization of the way work was managed. Henry Ford's famous assembly line was foreshadowed in the meat factories. One historian points out that already by 1870, "it took 157 men engaged in seventy-eight separate processes to take apart a steer" that would move down the line. Simons believed that workers could "perform the work equally well with eyes open or closed." The "disassembly line," as one historian later called it, captured a pattern of work that was spreading throughout the country at the time.

Not only was the meatpacking industry modern, it was perfectly set against the public interest. It was an equal opportunity exploiter. It paid the farmer and rancher less and less money for cattle, it mistreated the workers in the slaughterhouses by depressing their wages, and it covered up the quality of its products to the consumer. Anyone who paid attention to markets and prices would have noticed that, just as Sinclair was poised to investigate the stockyards, the price for cattle was going down, while the price of meat for consumers was going up. Sinclair couldn't have picked a more perfect target. . . .

Men Treated like Animals

The novel was not entirely a realist novel, because it was so infused with Sinclair's earlier romantic impulse. He called *The Jungle* the "result of an attempt to combine the best of two widely different schools; to put the content of [English poet Percy Bysshe] Shelley into the form of [French novelist Émile] Zola." It was also tinged by moralism, since Sinclair had wanted it to be "identical" with *Uncle Tom's Cabin*, the famous antislavery novel that tugged at the sentimentalism of the American middle class to show how inhumane the peculiar institution of slavery really was. Like [its author,] Harriet Beecher Stowe, Sinclair yanked at his readers' heartstrings, piling one episode of tragedy on top of the other and turning his characters into the passive victims of lascivious exploiters.

The Jungle tells the story of Jurgis, a Lithuanian immigrant to America who believes in pulling himself up by his own bootstraps. He believes that he will prevail, and the story that unravels shows how everything is stacked against him. Jurgis desperately struggles throughout the novel to keep his family together and uses any available contacts—a deli owner who got the family housing and jobs, for instance—to get by. When Jurgis finds a job, he is thrilled. But instead of achieving self-sufficiency, Jurgis discovers men who are treated like animals. Sinclair compared the animals being shipped in for slaughter to the men doing the killing, men separated from one another based on their individual tasks in a vast division of labor. Workers lacked a sense of the overall slaughtering process, and managers turned this to their advantage by speeding up each stage of the process. They could require "the same work in a shorter time, and paying the same wages, and then, after the workers had accustomed themselves to this new speed, they would reduce the rate of payment to correspond with the re-duction in time." Workers also learned how to turn their eyes from the awful things they were doing, like watching sickly cattle labeled unfit for consumption pass through the slaugh-terhouse anyway. They also noticed rats and how poison was set out to kill the rats, and then how the whole mess was ground up and shipped out to the consumer in the form of different meat products.

The Reality of Jurgis's American Dream

Jurgis's salvation from all this was found in his family, and the book documents his marriage and the birth of his first son and the purchase of something he thought he could only dream of, his own home. But then Sinclair documents how these sources of pride for Jurgis become sources of pain. Rav-enous real estate dealers trick Jurgis into signing bad agree-ments. He's stuck with a punitive mortgage. He then drinks away his grief in saloons whose owners feed on his limited supplies of cash. And then the rapacious forces of industrial capitalism destroy the family. His wife is forced into prostitution. In telling these stories, Sinclair hammers home his message: for immigrants like Jurgis, exploitation doesn't occur only at work, but in all areas of life. This was Horatio Alger [American writer of rags-to-riches tales] in reverse, going from down to lower down.

When Jurgis is injured, Sinclair brilliantly shows how something that might seem to be a small event can turn big quickly. Jurgis has no net to capture him when he falls through the cracks of the industry, and so after missing work and growing weak, Jurgis becomes unemployed and desperate. He sinks to the rank of fertilizer man, the lowest rung in the workplace hierarchy; and at the same time, his wife gets sick. She lies about her forced prostitution, and when Jurgis finds out, he assaults the factory boss who preyed upon his wife. With no legal defense, Jurgis lands in jail. While he is incarcerated, his house is repossessed, leaving Jurgis to feel like "the victim of ravenous vultures that had torn into his vitals and devoured him." His wife, growing sicker by the day and now nine months pregnant, dies in childbirth, along with the infant she was carrying. The dark details start piling on faster and faster, with Jurgis blacklisted from work and then his son drowning in the unpaved streets of a neighborhood with no sewers.

Jurgis travels to the country in order to escape, becoming a "tramp." Pulling away from the society he was once trapped in, Jurgis starts to gain perspective, and so too does the reader, who begins to see what Sinclair meant by the term "the jungle." "He saw the world of civilization then more plainly than ever he had seen it before; a world in which nothing counted but brutal might." He returns to the city when the weather turns cold, and he witnesses the hierarchy of class when taken to the home of a wealthy drunk. Though the wealthy man gives him some money, a well-connected barkeeper steals it. After fighting the barkeeper, Jurgis lands in jail again, where he learns how to live a life of crime, only to return to the "hog killing room" of his past. He joins a union and then takes part in the strike that had originally propelled Sinclair's interest—the strike of 1904. But Jurgis switches to become a scab. Seeing Connor, the man who led his wife to prostitution, he lashes out again, only to become an "outcast and a tramp once more." And soon thereafter, Jurgis is destitute again.

Sinclair drew his characters into a pit, creating an almost over-the-top description of human destruction. The novel became trapped in its own internal logic of desperation. But Sinclair could not end here, so he has Jurgis wander into a meeting where he hears the words of a socialist speaker. Sinclair projects the religious quality of his own conversion to socialism onto Jurgis. "There was a falling in of all the pillars of his soul," Sinclair explained, "the sky seemed to split above him." Jurgis is left to whisper, "By God! By God!" He is "converted to Socialism" in a way that's described as "supernatural." He starts to read [the socialist newspaper] *The Appeal to Reason*, full of "ginger and spice, of Western slang and hustle," and of course the paper where *The Jungle* was originally serialized. Jurgis now believes in the "cooperative commonwealth" made up of "self-governing communities." The book ends with hopefulness about socialism's growth and then climaxes in a rabble-rousing speech that was likely lifted from one of [socialist politician] Eugene Debs's. . . .

A Disappointing Impact

Reading the book, it's hard to miss its romantic passion to convert readers to socialism, but its intentions were muddied by the realities of history. The book entered a world not of its author's own making or under his control. Sinclair would famously state that he aimed for America's heart but hit its stomach. Yet at the time, he knew full well that the descriptions of the meatpacking industry's lack of cleanliness would make an impact. How could he imagine differently when he had written about "piles of meat" with "dried dung of rats" on top of them, and about how there was "no place for the men to wash their hands before they ate their dinner," so workers would wash "them in the water that was to be ladled into the sausage"? How could passages like these not turn the stomachs of Americans and make them demand something be done?

That's exactly what happened. Teddy Roosevelt read the book and quickly summoned Sinclair to the White House. Roosevelt knew the slop that passed for meat, having eaten military rations during the Spanish-American War that made him retch. But he needed his own investigators to check out the situation. Fearing delay, Sinclair quickly dispatched his investigator, Ella Reeve Bloor, to ensure that Roosevelt's boys wouldn't be misled by the meat industry. They weren't. The only thing they could not confirm was Sinclair's report that men fell into vats and wound up on the tables of beef-eating Americans. Sinclair knew that the families who had experienced this had been paid off, so he was not surprised that the rumors couldn't be proven.

As he watched the president, Sinclair came to believe that Teddy Roosevelt was "an aggressive and fearless servant of the general welfare" who had a "genius for publicity." But he still trusted his own sense of these things more. When he learned that Roosevelt's investigators had confirmed his novel's details, Sinclair rushed to the *New York Times*, where the editor supposedly screamed out "Stop the presses!" to include Sinclair's news in the next day's paper. Whether this story was true or not, the report went all over the place. Meat sales plummeted. People were talking about the book throughout the country. The public had awakened, and now it started demanding that something be done. So too did Sinclair, who kept writing

Roosevelt to do more. Roosevelt had to tell Sinclair that it was he who ran the country, not a lowly muckraker. . . .

It should come as no surprise to find that Sinclair was disappointed with the way things worked out. He believed that the solution to the problems outlined in *The Jungle* had to be total. Investigations were not enough; socialism was the only cure. Sinclair espoused the "municipal slaughterhouse" that was popular in some European countries. He believed government inspectors would be pushed around by the meat industry, as he himself showed them to be in *The Jungle*. Thus, the slaughterhouses should be operated for the public interest by the government itself. Sinclair called the Beveridge Bill "admirable" but said it wasn't stringent enough toward those who violated it. This was typical of Sinclair, this all-or-nothing attitude. And it represented his desire to embrace utopia over the practical reforms that Roosevelt believed in.

The Jungle's Realism Undermines Its Socialist Message

Christopher Hitchens

British journalist Christopher Hitchens has written for Vanity Fair. *He is the author of more than twenty books, including* Unacknowledged Legislation: Writers in the Public Sphere.

In The Jungle, *Upton Sinclair's realistic presentation of life in the Chicago stockyards is so powerful that it deflects attention from his socialist message. Instead, the story draws attention to unsanitary meatpacking practices, which captured the public's attention more powerfully than Sinclair's investigation of wage slavery and unfair labor practices. Similarly, the realistic, racist depiction of African American scabs detracts from the ideals of socialism expressed by proponents such as politician Eugene Debs. Finally, Sinclair's fascination with the meatpacking industry's dynamic and productive energy as seen in his extensive descriptions amounts to a celebration of capitalism, rather than an attack on it.*

Like [English novelist Charles] Dickens and [French novelist Émile] Zola, Upton Sinclair was in many ways a journalist. His greatest novel was originally commissioned as a serial, for the popular socialist paper *Appeal to Reason*, which was published (this now seems somehow improbable) in Kansas. An advance of $500 sent Sinclair to Chicago in 1904, there to make radical fiction out of brute reality. The city was then the great maw of American capitalism. That is to say, it took resources and raw materials from everywhere and convened them into money at an unprecedented rate. Hogs and steers, coal and iron, were transmuted into multifarious products by new and ruthless means. The Chicago system created almost every imaginable kind of goods. But the main thing it consumed was people. Upton Sinclair tried to elucidate and illuminate the ways in which commodities deposed, and controlled, human beings. His novel is the most successful attempt ever made to fictionalize the central passages of [Karl] Marx's *Das Kapital*.

Hard Times for Jurgis

The influence of Dickens can be felt in two ways. First, we are introduced to a family of naive but decent Lithuanian immigrants, sentimentally portrayed at a wedding feast where high hopes and good cheer provide some protection against the cruelty of quotidian [daily] life. There are lavishly spread tables, vital minor characters, and fiddle music. Second, we see these natural and spontaneous people being steadily reduced, as in [Dickens's novel] *Hard Times*, by crass utilitarian calculation. They dwell in a place named Packingtown, and "steadily reduced" is a euphemism. The extended family of the stolid Jurgis is exposed to every variety of misery and exploitation, and discovers slowly—necessarily slowly—that the odds are so arranged that no honest person can ever hope to win. The landlord, the saloonkeeper, the foreman, the shopkeeper, the ward heeler, all are leagued against the gullible toiler in such a way that he can scarcely find time to imagine what his actual employer or boss might be getting away with. To this accumulation of adversity Jurgis invariably responds with the mantra "I will work harder."

This is exactly what the innocent cart horse, Boxer, later says as he wears out his muscles on the cynical futilities of [George Orwell's] *Animal Farm*. Orwell was an admirer of Sinclair's work, and wrote in praise of *The Jungle* in 1940, but

Sinclair may have been depressed to see his main character redeployed in the service of allegory.

Sinclair's Realism

Sinclair's realism, indeed, got in the way of his socialism, in more than one fashion. His intention was to direct the conscience of America to the inhuman conditions in which immigrant labor was put to work. However, so graphic and detailed were his depictions of the filthy way in which food was produced that his book sparked a revolution among consumers instead (and led at some remove to the passage of the Food and Drugs Act and the Meat Inspection Act of 1906). He wryly said of this unintended consequence that he had aimed for the public's heart but had instead hit its stomach.

> There would be meat stored in great piles in rooms; and the water from leaky roofs would drip over it, and thousands of rats would race about on it. It was too dark in these storage places to see well but a man could run his hand over these piles of meat and sweep off handfuls of the dried dung of rats. These rats were nuisances, and the packers would put poisoned bread out for them; they would die, and then rats, bread, and meat would go into the hoppers together. This is no fairy story and no joke; the meat would be shovelled into carts, and the man who did the shovelling would not trouble to lift out a rat even when he saw one—there were things that went into the sausage in comparison with which a poisoned rat was a tidbit.

To this Sinclair added well-researched observations about the adulteration of food with chemicals and coloring. He also spared a thought, as did many of his later readers, for the animals themselves, especially (and ironically, in view of *Animal Farm*) for the pigs.

> At the head there was a great iron wheel, about twenty feet in circumference, with rings here and there along its edge.

Upon both sides of this wheel was a narrow space, into which came the hogs ... [Men] had chains which they fastened about the leg of the nearest hog, and the other end of the chain they hooked into one of the rings upon the wheel. So, as the wheel turned, a hog was suddenly jerked off his feet and borne aloft.

At the same instant the ear was assailed by a most terrifying shriek ... And meantime another [hog] was swung up, and then another, and another, until there was a double line of them, each dangling by a foot and kicking in frenzy—and squealing ... It was too much for some of the visitors—the men would look at each other, laughing nervously, and the women would stand with hands clenched, and the blood rushing to their faces, and the tears starting in their eyes.

Meantime, heedless of all these things, the men upon the floor were going about their work. Neither squeals of hogs nor tears of visitors made any difference to them; one by one they hooked up the hogs, and one by one with a swift stroke they slit their throats.

Again, the demands of verisimilitude [trueness to life] have a tendency to work against the recruitment of any sympathy for the calloused and even brutalized laborer. Sinclair's title, *The Jungle*, along with indirectly evoking the ideology of [British philosopher] Thomas Hobbes, inverts anthropomorphism by making men into brutes. ... [Critic] Jane Jacobs dwells on the passage above and on the sinister implications of machine civilization without registering what to me seems an obvious point: Sinclair was unconsciously prefiguring the industrialization of the mass slaughter of human beings—the principle of the abattoir [slaughter house] applied to politics and society by the degraded experimenters of the assembly line.

Protesting Wage Slavery

Eugene Debs, the great Socialist Party leader and orator of that period, announced that his ambition was to be "the John

A hog being stuck—bled to death while suspended from a conveyor belt—at Armour's meat packing plant in Chicago, 1893. The Library of Congress.

Brown [the radical Civil War abolitionist] of the wage slaves." This noble hyperbole was not all that much of an exaggeration: the lower orders in Chicago may have come voluntarily, to escape a Russian or a Polish house of bondage, rather than being brought by force from Africa *to* a house of bondage; but once here they were given only enough to keep them alive until their bodies wore out. Their children were exploited too, and their womenfolk were sexually vulnerable to the overseers. Indeed, the most wrenching section of the book comes in the middle, when Jurgis discovers that his wife has been preyed upon, under threat of dismissal, by a foreman. Not following the socialist script in the least, he sacrifices self-interest for pride and pounds the foreman to a pulp. By this means he swiftly discovers what side the courts and the cops and the laws are on, and is made to plumb new depths of degradation in prison. Among other humiliations, he stinks incurably from the materials of the plant, and offends even his fellow inmates. (We are not spared another Dickensian moment when he realizes that he has been jailed for the Christmas holidays and is overwhelmed by childhood memories.) Sinclair interrupts himself at this point to quote without attribution from [British writer Oscar Wilde's poem] *The Ballad of Reading Gaol* (Oscar Wilde was not long dead in 1905), and it seems a sure thing that Sinclair would have read [Wilde's essay] "The Soul of Man Under Socialism," the most brilliant line of which says that it is *capitalism* that lays upon men "the sordid necessity of living for others."

Robert Tressell's novel *The Ragged Trousered Philanthropists* (1914) is the only rival to *The Jungle* in its combination of realism with didacticism [instructional quality] and its willingness to impose a bit of theory on the readership. In both "proletarian" novels the weapon often deployed is satire: the workers are too dumb, and too grateful for their jobs, to consider the notions that might emancipate them.

Jurgis had no sympathy with such ideas as this—he could do the work himself, and so could the rest of them, he declared, if they were good for anything. If they couldn't do it, let them go somewhere else. Jurgis had not studied the books, and he would not have known how to pronounce "laissez-faire"; but he had been round the world enough to know that a man has to shift for himself in it, and that if he sets the worst of it, there is nobody to listen to him holler.

But gradually, after being for so long the anvil and not the hammer, he awakes from his bovine [cowlike] stupor and comes to understand that he has striven only to enrich others.

The book ends with the soaring notes of a socialist tribune of the people, and the triumphant yell—thrice repeated—"Chicago will be ours."

Racism in *The Jungle*

Before this happy ending, however, there is a passage that I am surprised Jane Jacobs does not discuss. A bitter strike is in progress in the stockyards, and gangs of scabs are being mobilized. They are from the South, and they are different. Indeed, the reader is introduced to "young white girls from the country rubbing elbows with big buck negroes with daggers in their boots, while rows of woolly heads peered down from every window of the surrounding factories."

> The ancestors of these black people had been savages in Africa; and since then they had been chattel slaves, or had been held down by a community ruled by the traditions of slavery. Now for the first time they were free, free to gratify every passion, free to wreck themselves . . .

This is no slip of the pen on Sinclair's part. He elsewhere refers to "a throng of stupid black negroes," a phrasing that convicts him of pleonasm [use of more words than are necessary to express a meaning] as well as of racism. It is often forgotten that the early American labor movement preached a sort of "white socialism" and—though Debs himself didn't subscribe to it—that this sadly qualified its larger claim to be the liberator of the wage slaves.

Unwittingly Celebrating Capitalism

The final way in which Sinclair's realism got the better of his socialism is this: like [German philosopher] Karl Marx in *The Communist Manifesto*, he couldn't help being exceedingly impressed by the dynamic, innovative, and productive energy of capitalism:

No tiniest particle of organic matter was wasted in Durham's. Out of the horns of the cattle they made combs, buttons, hair-pins, and imitation ivory; out of the shin bones and other big bones they cut knife and tooth-brush handles, and mouthpieces for pipes; out of the hoofs they cut hair-pins and buttons, before they made the rest into glue. From such things as feet, knuckles, hide clippings, and sinews came such strange and unlikely products as gelatin, isinglass, and phosphorus, bone-black, shoe-blacking, and bone oil. They had curled-hair works for the cattle-tails, and a "wool-pullery" for the sheep-skins; they made pepsin from the stomachs of the pigs, and albumen from the blood, and violin strings from the ill-smelling entrails. When there was nothing else to be done with a thing, they first put it into a tank and got out of it all the tallow and grease, and then they made it into fertilizer.

This account of the magnificent profusion that results from the assembly line and the division of labor is so awe-inspiring that Sinclair seems impelled to follow it almost at once with a correct and ironic discourse on the nature of monopoly and oligopoly: "So guileless was he, and ignorant of the nature of business, that he did not even realize that he had become an employee of Brown's, and that Brown and Durham were supposed by all the world to be deadly rivals— were even required to be deadly rivals by the law of the land, and ordered to try to ruin each other under penalty of fine and imprisonment!"

The Twenty-First-Century Jungle

Thus, though it lives on many a veteran's bookshelf as a stirring monument to the grandeur of the American socialist and labor movements, *The Jungle* may also be read today as a primer on the versatility of the capitalist system. But not all its "morals" belong to the past. The anti-Jungle ethos lived on, in a subterranean fashion, through the League for Industrial Democracy, founded by Sinclair and [American author] Jack

London. (Its junior branch, the Student League for Industrial Democracy, survived long enough to provide the auspices for the first meeting of [the radical political group] Students for a Democratic Society.) In Eric Schlosser's best seller *Fast Food Nation* (2001) the values and practices of the slaughterhouse system were revisited. Most of the reviews, rather predictably, concentrated on the shock effect of Schlosser's intimate— almost intestinal—depiction of "hamburger" ingredients. But Schlosser also spent a great deal of time with those whose lives are lived at the point of production. Recruited, often illegally, from the Central American isthmus rather than the Baltic littoral [shores], these workers are sucked into cutting machines, poisoned by chemicals, and made wretched by a pervasive stench that won't wash off. Their wages are low, their hours long, their conditions arduous, and their job security nonexistent. The many women among them are considered bounty by lascivious supervisors, who sometimes dangle the prospect of green cards or safer jobs, and sometimes don't bother even to do that. The health-and-safety inspectors are about as vigilant and incorruptible as they were a century ago. The main difference is that these plants are usually located in remote areas or rural states, so the consolations of urban and communal solidarity are less available to the atomized work force than they were to Jurgis and his peers. This nonfiction work is also a blow to the national gut; but if properly read, it might succeed where *The Jungle* failed, and bring our stomachs and our hearts—and even our brains—into a better alignment.

Sinclair's Depiction of African American Strikebreakers Is Racist

Mark Noon

Mark Noon has taught at Bloomsburg University of Pennsylvania. He is the author of a series of labor-related entries in the Encyclopedia of American Social Movements *and the* Historical Encyclopedia of American Labor.

Because unions often discriminated against African American laborers, such workers often found themselves in the role of strikebreakers, or "scabs." These black strikebreakers are cast in the role of villain in the fiction of social realists such as Upton Sinclair. During the worker strike that takes place in The Jungle, *Jurgis is put in charge of a group of African American strikebreakers. These men are described in negative, demeaning terms with regard to their abilities, personal habits, and work ethic. Additionally, while Sinclair describes violence against whites in graphic detail throughout the novel, violent episodes in which African Americans figure as victims are minimized.*

> I wonder why
>
> They are so shortsighted
>
> As not to realize
>
> That every time
>
> They keep any worker,
>
> man or woman,
>
> White, yellow, or black,

Mark Noon, "'It ain't your color, it's your scabbing': Literary Depictions of African American Strikebreakers," *African-American Review*, vol. 38, no. 3, 2004, pp. 429–439. Copyright © 2004 Mark Noon. Reproduced by permission of the author.

OUT of a UNION,

They are forcing a worker

To be a SCAB,

To be used AGAINST THEM?

> —*from "The Negro Worker"*

These lines of verse, published in *The Messenger* in July 1919, make a point about strikes that is frequently disregarded in the hundreds of pages of fiction by social realists who addressed the major labor struggles of the late nineteenth and early twentieth centuries: "[A]ny worker / man or woman, / White, yellow, or black" could be a strikebreaker. In the West, for example, railroad and mining company managers used workers from countries such as China, Italy, Greece, Japan, and Mexico to break strikes, fully aware that these immigrants would have no allegiance to the ethnic groups who had thrown down their tools in protest. Surprisingly, strikebreaking even crossed class lines as upper and middle class male college students also took on the role of strike-breaker to express their antagonism toward workers. The variety of sources of strikebreakers is not fully reflected in the fictional response to the strike. In some of the most significant radical fiction of the early twentieth century, black workers—more than any other group—are curiously cast in the villainous role of "scab." . . .

Union Discrimination

Ample evidence of friction between whites and blacks can be found in some of the U.S. labor movement's key strikes in the late nineteenth and early twentieth centuries. The use of black troops offers the earliest examples. Black soldiers were used against striking miners in Coeur d'Alene, Idaho, in 1892 and 1899, because African Americans "were believed much less likely than white troops to fraternize with the strikers." In addition, black troops guarded trains and railroad property during the Pullman Strike of 1894. Regarding African American civilians, the Knights of Labor and the newly developing American Federation of Labor (AFL) successfully attracted African American workers, and examples of interracial unity both in the workplace and during strikes can be found. But as the lines from "The Negro Worker" also imply, some unions excluded black members. If blacks were welcomed as members, they faced discriminatory policies under a second-class status. Blacks were denied work on union projects despite membership, or they were denied better jobs despite seniority. Unions failed to protect blacks from racial hostility, and blacks charged union leaders with ignoring their complaints of discrimination. The development of segregated locals was another sign of trouble. Before the Civil War, [black writer, orator, and abolitionist] Frederick Douglass wrote in favor of labor unity between African American and white workers; however, when he realized that labor was doing little to lessen racial animosity, he came out in favor of blacks taking the jobs of strikers: "Colored men can feel under no obligation to hold out in a 'strike' with the whites, as the latter have never recognized them." As America's industrial revolution picked up steam, this issue came into greater prominence in most mass production industries in cities in the North. Racism fueled an African American labor force ready and willing to break strikes.

African Americans in *The Jungle*

One of the earliest and most significant fictional treatments of African American strikebreakers is found in Upton Sinclair's *The Jungle* (1906). The labor struggle in the canonical novel is based on the unsuccessful stockyard strike by thousands of packinghouse workers and mechanical tradesmen of the Amalgamated Meat Cutters and Butcher Workmen in Chicago in 1904. African Americans had been used as strikebreakers in the meat packing industry at least as early as 1894, in response to a sympathy strike by packing and slaughterhouse workers who supported Eugene Debs and the American Railway Union during the Pullman Strike. Sinclair, who covered the 1904 strike as a journalist for the Socialist weekly *Appeal to Reason*, was among an increasing number of pro-labor social realists exposed to the problems of the working class through journalism. But he apparently had little sympathy for the struggles of African Americans, as his racist depiction of the strikebreakers makes clear.

As the strike develops in *The Jungle*, Sinclair accurately reflects the historical record by demonstrating that strikebreakers were racially and ethnically mixed. The novel's protagonist, Lithuanian Jurgis Rudkus, is among the workers who decide to cross the picket lines as well as "the lowest foreigners—Greeks, Roumanians, Sicilians, and Slovaks." In fact, Rudkus is placed in charge of the strikebreakers—a group described by Sinclair as "a throng of stupid black Negroes, and foreigners who could not understand a word that was said to them." Sinclair portrays the strikebreakers—particularly the African Americans—as lazy, incompetent, and threatening—especially when they get access to knives in the packinghouse. *The Jungle* details the pathetic attempt by Rudkus to "teach" the strikebreakers in order to increase production on the killing floor:

> He had not the most tractable pupils, however. "See hyar, boss," a big black "buck" would begin, "ef you doan' like de way Ah does dis job, you kin get somebody else to do it." Then a crowd would gather and listen, muttering threats. After the first meal nearly all the steel knives had been missing, and now every Negro had one, ground to a fine point, hidden in his boot.

Due to the chaos and tension in the plant, management is unable to meet the demands of the meat market and is forced into a doomed attempt at arbitration. The packers then attempt to replace the striking workers permanently with "gangs of Negroes in the country districts of the far South."

Sinclair Discredits Blacks

A tactic used by capital against labor is to emphasize the criminal element among *strikers*, ignoring the fact that most were law-abiding citizens. Sinclair utilizes this technique against capitalism by tagging *strikebreakers* with vice, immorality, and criminality; however, he explicitly associates these characteristics with African Americans as a group. He discredits blacks through what [historian] Eugene Leach labels "mob stigma" and "hostile generalizations," using "well-established metaphoric conventions that characterized mobs as natural forces—volcanoes, storms, wild animal herds—which degraded human beings." Sinclair writes in *The Jungle* that "the vast majority [of strikebreakers] were 'green' Negroes from the cotton districts of the far South, and they were herded into the packing-plants like sheep." More viciously, he writes:

> [A]nd any night, in the big open space in front of Brown's one might see brawny Negroes stripped to the waist and pounding each other for money, while a howling throng of three or four thousand surged about, men and women, young white girls from the country rubbing elbows with big buck Negroes with daggers in their boots, while rows of woolly heads peered down from every window of the surrounding factories. The ancestors of these black people had been savages in Africa; and since then they had been chattel slaves, or had been held down by a community ruled by the traditions of slavery. Now for the first time they were free,—free to gratify every passion, free to wreck themselves. They were wanted to break a strike, and when it was broken they would be shipped away, and their present masters would never see them again, and so whiskey and women were brought in by the car-load and sold to them, and hell was loose in the yards.

Sinclair's repeated references to African American men as "bucks" are significant. In a study of the stereotypes of African Americans in film, Donald Bogle notes that the character of the black buck or black brute appears in D. W. Griffith's controversial *The Birth of a Nation*. Bogle describes the figure as "subhuman . . . nameless characters setting out on a rampage of black rage. Bucks are always big, baaadd [*sic*] niggers, over-sexed and savage, violent and frenzied as they lust for white flesh." Sinclair offers a similar stereotype, dramatizing the accusation by union officials in Chicago that African American strikebreakers brought immoral conditions to the plants because they were more libidinous than white workers. The lack of objection to racist passages provides additional proof that American socialists were influenced by a doctrine of white supremacy during this time, a doctrine which argued "that the Negro belonged to an inferior race and warned their comrades against violating the Caucasian purity of their association." The image of African Americans as a "scab race" was evident in other circles as well: "Racist politicians and union leaders helped mold this perception, as witnessed by . . . AFL official John Roach, who described the black scabs as 'huge strapping fellows, ignorant and vicious, whose predominating trait was animalism.'"

Violence Against African Americans

While it has been noted that strikebreakers were racially and ethnically mixed during the stockyard strikes, the historical record indicates that acts of hatred and violence were particularly harsh when directed against African Americans:

> Effigies with the words 'Nigger Scab' scrawled upon them hung from lamp-posts around the stockyards. . . . An angry mob mauled a black laborer and his ten-year-old son; another black lost both eyes when caught by a crowd of enraged whites. At least one black worker was stabbed to death, and others were reported to have been drowned in the fetid

waters of "Bubbly Creek" north of the yards. At times, the violence assumed a generalized character, as whites attacked any black unlucky enough to be found in the vicinity of the plants.

While Sinclair does not ignore the violence against strikebreakers in his fictional treatment of the subject, on this point he reduces the degree of historical specificity. In one scene, for example, when Jurgis and three other workers go outside the stockyard in search of alcohol and are chased by strikers as "scabs," a scuffle ensues. The incident is blown out of proportion in the newspapers, as Sinclair attempts to impress upon the reader the press's tendency to exaggerate strike-related violence. Later in the chapter, Sinclair again minimizes the violence against African American strikebreakers by simply noting that the "scab" who made the mistake of wandering into Packingtown "fared badly." *The Jungle* also disregards the historical record and never indicates that many blacks were faithful to union causes and opted not to cross picket lines. . . .

The Jungle's Conclusion Weakens Sinclair's Message About Workers' Rights

Walter B. Rideout

Walter B. Rideout taught at Northwestern University and the University of Wisconsin. He is the editor of numerous texts, including A College Book of Modern Verse *and* A College Book of Modern Fiction.

Upton Sinclair drew inspiration from numerous sources while writing The Jungle. *Growing up in poverty helped him to understand the plight of wage slaves in Chicago's Packingtown. From religion, he gained the notion of following Christ's teachings about caring for the poor and loving all men as brothers. His discovery of socialism led directly to his writing* The Jungle. *Many critics have found fault with Jurgis Rudkus's similar conversion to socialism. Though Sinclair foreshadows Jurgis's change of heart well, it is not as powerfully portrayed as his previous victimization at the hands of the meatpacking industry. Sinclair's message is weakened when, at its conclusion, the novel becomes an intellectualized socialist essay.*

When *The Jungle* appeared in book form [in 1906], even the conservative literary critics agreed, with certain reservations, that at last an American was painting a picture "of those sunk in the innermost depths of the modern [Dante's] *Inferno.*" Part of the novel's abrupt success among the public at large may have resulted, as Sinclair himself was to lament, from the unintended relevance of a brief muckraking passage on filthy meat; but no novel is read because of half a dozen pages, and this one was read internationally. The extent of the young writer's popularity is suggested by the remark of [Danish critic] Georg Brandes, on his visit to the United States eight years later, that the three modern American novelists he found worth reading were Frank Norris, Jack London, and Upton Sinclair.

Europeans continue [in the 1950s] to read Upton Sinclair . . . , even if European critics on tour to the United States have long since ceased to speak of him; but it is now impossible for a citizen of the prophet's own country to go through Sinclair's work—the earlier novels as well as the . . . nonstop flight with Lanny Budd [the hero of a series of Sinclair's novels] across recent history—without a mixed feeling of impatience and respect: impatience with him as a writer for his refusal, or inability, to make a final imaginative fusion of material and purpose; respect for him as a person, despite his curiously impersonal egoism, because of his generosity, his openness of heart, his courage, and his devotion to truth as he sees it.

The Influence of Poverty

The author of *The Jungle* was born in Baltimore in 1878 of a father and mother impoverished by the economic dislocations of the postbellum South, yet proud in their family ancestries. Through his father he was descended from a line of officers who had served with distinction in the British and American navies—seven Sinclairs had also been officers in the Confederate Navy—while his mother's family was a moderately wealthy one; but Sinclair's father, a liquor salesman, as one of his own best, or worst, customers, was unable to support his family, and slowly and terribly drank himself to death. Sinclair later explained in his book of reminiscences, *American Outpost*, that one of his reasons for becoming a social rebel was his psychology as a "poor relation."

Readers of my novels know that I have one favorite theme, the contrast of the social classes; there are characters from both worlds, the rich and the poor, and the plot is contrived to carry you from one to the other. The explanation of this literary phenomenon is that, from the first days I can remember, my life was a series of Cinderella transformations; one night sleeping on a vermin-ridden sofa in a lodging-house, and the next night under silken coverlets in a fashionable home. It was always a question of one thing— whether my father had the money for that week's board. If he didn't, my mother paid a visit to her father, the railroad official.

The Influence of Religion, Literature, and Socialism

A second influence that assisted in guiding him ultimately to revolt was, Sinclair maintains, the Protestant Episcopal Church, since he "took the words of Jesus seriously," envisioning himself as a follower of "the rebel carpenter, the friend of the poor and lowly, the symbol of human brotherhood." Although he early lost faith in Christianity as anything more than a code of ethics, Sinclair has characteristically continued to hold Jesus as one of his heroes. In his own battle for Truth against Evil, he has made his life one long saga of [English legendary hero] St. George and the Dragon. An intense, sensitive boy, he was shocked into an ascetic denial of all indulgences by the decline and death of his father, whom he stood by loyally and through whose sufferings he discovered an important social fact, that behind the saloon-keeper loomed the politicians and Big Business. Disgusted with the ugliness of the world, he turned for escape to literature, where he found his spirit of revolt so strengthened that he came to suppose that literature made life. Like his character Thyrsis in [his] semiautobiographical [novel] *Love's Pilgrimage*, he read [Spanish writer Miguel de Cervantes'] *Don Quixote* and [French writer Victor Hugo's] *Les Miserables*; he loved [English novelist] George

Eliot and was thrilled by the social protest of [English author Charles] Dickens; he admired [English novelist William] Thackeray most of all, for Thackeray saw the human corruption which lay at the heart of the world that he described. Significantly, the boy's favorite poets were the blind [English poet John] Milton and the revolutionary [English poet Percy Bysshe] Shelley.

Two elements in the education of this social rebel still remained to take effect. The first was a prolonged acquaintance with what he later called "the economic screw." He supported himself for a year of graduate work at Columbia [University in New York] by hack writing, producing thousands of words of boys' stories each week. Then he broke away to write the Great American Novel, married the adoring Meta Fuller, and endured with her several years of drudging poverty, desperately trying to publish his first novels and performing more hack work in order to keep his wife and newly-born son alive. In the autumn of 1902 he was rescued from this marginal existence by the kindness of George D. Herron, a gentle-minded Socialist writer and lecturer, who gave him financial support and, equally important in Sinclair's development, helped him to discover Socialism. Reading *Wilshire's* [magazine] completed the conversion. Sinclair had more years of the economic screw to endure, but now he could gird himself for the fight with the whole armor of an economic and political philosophy.

> It was like the falling down of prison walls about my mind; the most amazing discovery, after all these years—that I did not have to carry the whole burden of humanity's future upon my two frail shoulders! There were actually others who understood; who saw what had gradually become clear to me, that the heart and centre of the evil lay in leaving the social treasure, which nature had created, and which every man has to have in order to live, to become the object of a scramble in the market-place, a delirium of speculation. The

principal fact which the Socialists had to teach me, was the fact that they themselves existed. . . .

Dedicated to Workingmen

The Jungle is dedicated "To the Workingmen of America." Into it had gone Sinclair's heartsick discovery of the filth, disease, degradation, and helplessness of the packing workers' lives. But any muckraker could have put this much into a book; the fire of the novel came from Sinclair's whole passionate, rebellious past, from the insight into the pattern of capitalist oppression shown him by Socialist theory, and from the immediate extension into the characters' lives of his own and his wife's struggle against hunger, illness, and fear. It was the summation of his life and experience into a manifesto. The title of the book itself represented a feat of imaginative compression, for the world in which the Lithuanian immigrant Jurgis and his family find themselves is an Africa of unintelligibility, of suffering and terror, where the strong beasts devour the weak, who are dignified, if at all, only by their agony. . . .

Jurgis's Conversion

The "conversion" pattern of *The Jungle* has been attacked as permitting too easy a dramatic solution; however, aside from the recognized fact that many conversions have occurred before and since [the Apostle] Paul saw the light on the road to Damascus, it should be noted that in *The Jungle* Sinclair carefully prepares such an outcome by conducting Jurgis through all the circles of the workers' inferno and by attempting to show that no other savior except Socialism exists. Perhaps a more valid objection to the book is Sinclair's failure to realize his characters as "living" persons, a charge which, incidentally, may be brought against many nonconversion novels. Jurgis is admittedly a composite figure who was given a heaping share of the troubles of some twenty or thirty packing workers with whom Sinclair had talked, and the author's psychology of character is indeed a simple one. Although in the introductory wedding scene Jurgis and the other major characters are sharply sketched as they had appeared to the writer at an actual wedding feast in Packingtown, during the remainder of the book they gradually lose their individuality, becoming instead any group of immigrants destroyed by the Beef Trust. Yet paradoxically, the force and passion of the book are such that this group of lay figures with Jurgis at their head, these mere capacities for infinite suffering, finally do come to stand for the masses themselves, for all the faceless ones to whom things are done. Hardly individuals, they nevertheless collectively achieve symbolic status.

Sinclair's success in creating this jungle world emphasizes by contrast what is actually the book's key defect. Jurgis's conversion is probable enough, the Socialist explanation might well flash upon him with the blinding illumination of a religious experience; but practically from that point onward to the conclusion of his novel Sinclair turns from fiction to another kind of statement. Where the capitalist damnation, the destruction of the immigrants, has been proved almost upon the reader's pulses, the Socialist salvation, after its initial impact, is intellectualized. The reader cannot exist imaginatively in Jurgis's converted state even if willing, for Jurgis hardly exists himself. What it means to be a Socialist is given, not through the rich disorder of felt experience, but in such arbitrarily codified forms as political speeches, an essay on Party personalities, or the long conversation in monologues about the Coöperative Commonwealth which comprises most of the book's final chapter. *The Jungle* begins and lives as fiction; it ends as a political miscellany.

The Failure of *The Jungle*'s Form and Message

The fact that Jurgis's militant acceptance of Socialism is far less creatively realized than his previous victimization is indicative of how Sinclair's outraged moral idealism is attracted more to the pathos than the power of the poor, and suggests his real affinity for the mid-Victorian [nineteenth-century] English reform novelists. More specifically, *The Jungle* is reminiscent of the work of the humanitarian Dickens, whose social protest had "thrilled" the young rebel. There are frequent resemblances between the two writers in narrative method, in presentation of character, in the tendency of both to intrude themselves with bubbling delight or horrified indignation into the scene described. Whole paragraphs on the wedding feast of Jurgis Rudkus and Ona recall, except for the Lithuanian, the manner of Dickens with the Cratchits' Christmas dinner [in *A Christmas Carol*], and Madame Haupt, fat, drunken, and filthy, might have been a midwife in *Oliver Twist*'s London. Finally, the temper of Sinclair's protest is curiously like that of Dickens. Where the latter urges only the literal practice of Christianity as a remedy for the cruelties he describes, Sinclair, to be sure, demands the complete transformation of the existing order of things by the Socialist revolution; yet the revolution that the orator so apocalyptically envisages at the conclusion to *The Jungle* is to be accomplished by the ballot and not by the bullet. Sinclair's spirit is not one of blood and barricades, but of humanitarianism and brotherly love.

Both in life and in writings Sinclair has attempted, as did Dickens, to be the persuading intermediary between the contending classes. With admirable sweetness of temper, considering his lack of success, he has continued to argue that the owning class should perform a revolution by consent, that the capitalist should give up his profits and power in exchange for citizenship in an industrial democracy. But in the novels that he has so prodigally brought forth year after year since the publication of *The Jungle*, the lamb of his Christian spirit has rarely been able peacefully to lie down with the lion of his Marxian [after the German philosopher Karl] vocabulary. As a result, although Sinclair is the only one of the Socialist novelists who continued . . . to write Socialist novels, his is the classic case among them for unresolved discrepancies between his fictional structure and the "message" that he is trying to convey. The formal flaw of *The Jungle* represents one such failure.

The Jungle Is Still Relevant

Bryan Hayes

Bryan Hayes works for MacNeil/Lehrer productions, which pro-
duces a nightly news show on the Public Broadcasting Service.

The one hundredth anniversary (in 2006) of the publication
of Sinclair's The Jungle *brought the book back into the public*
eye and raised the issue of whether true reform has taken place
in the meatpacking industry. While the 1906 publication of the
novel famously brought on reforms in the food industry and led
to the creation of the Food and Drug Administration, questions
remain as to whether industry workers have fared any better
than in Jurgis Rudkus's day. Today, many in the meatpacking
force are illegal immigrants. They are afraid to unionize, and
thus are subject to low wages and poor working conditions. Their
work is still dangerous and workers' injuries are often not re-
ported. While the American Meat Institute claims that condi-
tions are much better and that even Upton Sinclair would be
impressed, others say that despite improvements, the meatpack-
ing industry still has a long way to go.

Upton Sinclair's famous novel, "The Jungle," which graphically depicts the lives of slaughterhouse workers, turn[ed]
100 [in 2006]. Still required reading for many students, the
book examines issues about immigrant workers and the meat
industry that remain relevant today.

Life was tough for workers in the Chicago stockyards 100
years ago. Many of the workers came from Eastern Europe
and spoke little to no English. They waited in long lines hoping to be chosen for a few days' work.

Inside the factory, laborers were injured regularly in the
hot, bloody and greasy environment.

Bryan Hayes, "Sinclair's *The Jungle* Turns 100," *NewsHour Extra*, May 10, 2006.
www.pbs.org/newshour/extra. Copyright © 2006 MacNeil/Lehrer Productions. Reproduced by permission.

Back and shoulder injuries from heavy lifting and repetitive movements were common.

Among workers who handled knives Sinclair wrote that, "You could scarcely find a person who had the use of his thumb." Other workers were burnt and blinded by exposure to dangerous chemicals.

The meat factories also were unsanitary and infested with rats.

Before dying, poisoned rats would often climb into piles of meat, where they would end up in food sold to people, according to Sinclair's descriptions.

Sinclair's further graphic details of the slaughter of diseased animals, chemicals used to cover the smell of spoiled meat, and workers' using the workspace as a bathroom all led to public outrage.

Workplace Improvements

The book had a dramatic effect on the food industry: domestic and foreign purchases of American meat fell by half and people began to clamor for government action.

Six months after "The Jungle" was published, Congress passed the Meat Inspection Act and the Pure Food and Drug Act of 1906. These laws effectively created the Food and Drug Administration [FDA].

While the FDA continues to set and enforce standards for food production today, the U.S. Department of Agriculture is now in charge of inspecting slaughterhouses and meatpacking plants.

While it took less than a year to improve food safety, better working conditions took another 15 years.

When meat workers formed unions in the 1920s they were able to collectively bargain with company owners on bettering their working conditions.

A poster advertising The Jungle. The Library of Congress.

Still the most dangerous industrial job in the country, by the early 1980s meat workers' wages were up to $18 an hour, the highest paid for industrial work in the United States.

Extensive health benefits and retirement plans helped make the work more acceptable.

Changing Workforces: Illegal Immigrants

But by the mid-1980s, meatpacking companies relocated their plants from urban areas like Chicago to new state-of-the-art facilities in rural locales like North Carolina, Kansas and western Nebraska, where they were able to reduce costs.

Today the meatpacking workforce is largely made up of immigrants from Latin America. Charlie LeDuff, a reporter for *The New York Times*, says that these workers, many undocumented or illegal, are often the only people willing to work this job.

And because they're illegal they are reluctant to unionize, afraid they'll be deported.

"For their part, many of the Mexicans . . . fear that a union would place their illegal status under scrutiny and force them out," reported LeDuff, who went undercover as a meat worker in a pork plant in North Carolina.

Wages have fallen to between $8 to $12 an hour.

[In 2005], Human Rights Watch, a nonprofit organization looking to draw attention to human rights violations worldwide, issued a report criticizing the industry for increasing production at the cost of workers' health.

Working with fast-moving conveyor belts, employees must make hurried and repeated movements that make them susceptible "to constant, foreseeable and preventable risk of injury," according to Lance Compa, author of the report.

Many of the workers' injuries are not reported.

"Workers are under constant pressure from managers and supervisors not to report injuries (many managers get pay bonuses for low reporting rates), and fear losing their jobs if they report injuries. Immigrant workers especially are vulnerable to pressure not to file such reports," Compa said in an editorial, co-written with Jamie Fellner, that was published in the *Washington Post*.

A New Jungle

The American Meat Institute, which was founded in 1906, dismisses the claims in the report, saying "wages are competitive (about $25,000 a year), turnover is wildly exaggerated, and safety has dramatically improved."

J. Patrick Boyle, the institute's president, said in the last 15 years, the plants have invested in more power tools and better-designed work stations.

"It's a new world," he told the Associated Press [AP]. "If Upton Sinclair walked through our plants today, he'd say he was a successful reformer."

Others say even with better conditions, the meatpacking industry falls short when compared to progress made at other workplaces.

"It's a new 'Jungle,' measured not against the standard of yesterday, but the standard of today," said Lourdes Gouveia, director of the Office for Latino/Latin American Studies at the University of Nebraska at Omaha, according to the AP.

Upton Sinclair Was Wrong: The American Dream Is Alive

The Economist

When Upton Sinclair published The Jungle, *he believed he was promoting socialism. Instead, readers focused on the unsanitary conditions in slaughterhouses. But Sinclair has been proven wrong in many respects. Today the meatpacking industry has changed dramatically, and while working conditions may be somewhat dangerous, they are no more onerous than those of many other professions. Mexican immigrants, who now do the types of jobs at which Jurgis Rudkus once toiled, have bountiful economic opportunities, and many who get a foothold in low-paying, difficult jobs move on to owning their own businesses. These immigrants make the most of their opportunities, and, for many, the American dream is alive and well.*

[In 1906], a sensational novel attacking the meatpacking industry prompted Congress to draft the first federal food-safety laws. The author of "The Jungle", Upton Sinclair, was disappointed. He had hoped to persuade Americans to embrace socialism. For him, the important point was not that the slaughterhouses of Chicago were unsanitary, but that they were "the spirit of capitalism made flesh"—a system in which "a hundred human lives did not balance a penny of profit." The book's central character, a Lithuanian named Jurgis Rudkus, had come to America believing that through hard work he could grasp the American Dream. But he found that "the whole country . . . was nothing but one gigantic lie."

The Economist, "Of Meat, Mexicans and Social Mobility; Immigration and *The Jungle*," vol. 379, June 17, 2006, p. 32. Copyright © 2006 Economist Newspaper Ltd. Republished with permission of *The Economist*, conveyed through Copyright Clearance Center, Inc.

Sinclair Was Wrong About America

Rarely has a great novelist been so wrong about so much. No one now worries about the poverty of Lithuanian-Americans. But many still worry about the health of the American Dream. Can immigrants still work their way up from the bottom? Can they become American?

Many fear that, for the latest wave of mostly-unskilled immigrants from Latin America, the answer is no. Some fret that the newcomers are too ill-educated and culturally alien to prosper or assimilate. Others are convinced that immigrant workers are horribly exploited or trapped forever in low-wage jobs. Both worries are largely unfounded.

The New Meatpacking Industry

Consider Alberto Queiroz, who crept across the border [in 1996]. After a stuffy ride in the boot [trunk] of a car, he found his first job in a Chinese-owned clothes factory in Los Angeles. Workers with papers were paid the minimum wage, he recalls. Having none, he had to make do with $2.50 an hour. Though unlawfully stingy, this was much better than he could have earned back home in Mexico.

After two years he moved to North Carolina, a state that was then just starting to become a magnet for Mexicans. He picked blueberries for $5 a box, earning nearly $100, tax free, for a 12-hour day. But this job lasted only two months, until the harvest ended. So he sought more stable employment, which he eventually found at America's largest hog slaughterhouse.

Smithfield Foods' plant at Tar Heel, North Carolina, turns some 32,000 pigs a day into hams and loins. Thanks to selective breeding and efficient, hygienic processing, American meat has grown steadily leaner, cheaper and safer, says Joe Luter, Smithfield's chairman. A hundred years ago, food ate up half of Americans' take-home pay; now it is only about a tenth, and no one gets trichinosis from Mr Luter's pork chops.

But is a slaughterhouse a nice place to work? Smithfield does not let journalists in, for reasons of "biosecurity". Human Rights Watch, a watchdog from New York, issued a report in 2004 entitled "Blood, Sweat and Fear", which accused American meat and poultry firms of "systematic human-rights violations". Slaughterhouses are harsh and dangerous places to work, said the report, and illegal immigrants, who form a large chunk of the workforce, find it hard to defy abusive employers.

Mr Queiroz takes a more benign view. Yes, the work is hard. The line goes fast and you have to keep cutting till your hands are exhausted. And yes, it is sometimes dangerous. He says he once saw a co-worker lose a leg when he ducked under the disassembly line instead of walking round it. But many occupations are risky. Taxi-drivers are 34 times more likely to die on the job than meatpackers.

Mr Queiroz does not think Smithfield was a bad employer. Wages of more than $10 an hour enabled him to buy a house back in Mexico. Cutting up pigs was easier than picking blueberries, he says, because he did not have to toil under the sun all day. And when he had had enough, he quit and set up a taco stand with his brother. That was [in 2001]. Now he owns a Mexican restaurant. America, he says, is "the land of opportunity".

The meatpacking industry has changed dramatically since Sinclair's day, when pigs and cattle were transported live to city stockyards so that the meat would still be edible when city-dwellers bought it. Now, thanks to better roads and refrigerated trucks, there is no need to build slaughterhouses near where customers live. No pigs have been slaughtered in Chicago for years. Firms like Smithfield now favour rural sites, where rents and wages are lower. And the immigrant workforce is largely Hispanic, since Jurgis Rudkus's great-grandchildren prefer to work in offices.

The Benefits of Immigration

News about jobs spreads quickly through the Hispanic grapevine. The shift of meatpackers to the countryside is one of many market signals attracting immigrants to different parts of America. New migrants head not only for California, New York, Texas and Florida, but also for Georgia, Arizona, Arkansas and Oregon. Perhaps the most rapid change has taken place in North Carolina, where a technology and construction boom has sucked in hundreds of thousands of migrant workers, swelling the Hispanic population by more than 1,000% since 1990.

In some areas, the newcomers strain local services. Cindy Evans, director of a county clinic for children in Raleigh, says the percentage of her patients who are Hispanic has leapt from perhaps 2% a decade and a half ago to about 65%. The clinic is full of bilingual signs. Next to one, someone has scrawled: "Speak English!".

Many native-born North Carolinians are uneasy about the pace at which their state has Latinised. Few of the newcomers arrived legally. Some join gangs. As in the rest of America, antipathy towards illegal immigrants, though widespread, is mostly mild and seldom violent. It should not be dismissed, however, since it is politically influential. In Washington, Congress is still struggling to reconcile rival immigration reforms—a House bill that cracks down on illegals and a Senate bill that offers them a path to citizenship. Throughout the country, populists echo and stoke their constituents' anxieties.

Fear of immigration is akin to fear of globalisation. Unemployment may be low, but many Americans fear losing their jobs to someone cheaper in Bangalore, [India,] or someone who took the bus up from Tijuana. Meanwhile, the benefits of immigration, like those of globalisation, are often taken for granted. "Americans just assume they can have a pizza delivered for $9," says Federico van Gelderen, a Raleigh-based executive for Univision, a Spanish-language television station.

Accurately measuring the economic consequences of immigration is hard. Looking only at North Carolina, John Kasarda and James Johnson recently found that Latinos paid $756 [million] in taxes annually and cost the state government $817 [million]. That works out as a net burden of $102 per head. Anti-immigrant agitators will seize on this figure, worries Mr Kasarda, a professor at the University of North Carolina's Kenan-Flagler Business School. But it is dwarfed by the positive impact of Latino spending in North Carolina, which he estimates at $9.19 billion in 2004. That translates into nearly 90,000 new jobs, he says.

Upwardly Mobile Immigrants

The worry that America is importing a new Hispanic under-class, as some claim, is also probably unfounded. Granted, foreign-born Hispanics are less educated and earn less than the average American. But that is hardly surprising, given that so many were until recently Mexican peasants. What matters is whether they are socially mobile, and it seems that they are. Although, by some measures of income and education, the Hispanic average is not improving much, that average is dragged down by a steady influx of poor Mexicans. A better way of gauging progress is to look at inter-generational differences.

First-generation male Mexican immigrants earn only half as much as white men. But the second generation have overtaken black men and earn three-quarters as much as whites. They enjoy more benefits than the first generation, too: they are twice as likely to have employer-provided pensions and one-and-a-half times more likely to have health insurance.

And the adult daughters of Mexican immigrants, having learned English, are much more likely to have jobs than their mothers were.

Some economists, notably George Borjas of Harvard, grumble that "about half of the differences in relative economic status across ethnic groups observed in one generation persist into the next." Maybe so. But in absolute terms, Mexicans have grown much richer by coming to the United States. If they had not, they would go home. And their children are doing even better. Whereas only 40% of first-generation Mexican immigrants between the ages of 16 and 20 are in school or college, nearly two-thirds of the second generation are. Between the ages of 21 and 25 the leap is even more striking, from 7.3% to 24.4%.

For many first-generation immigrants, getting their children into an American university is the final proof that they have made it. Marco Roldan, for example, has been in America for 22 years but still has a Guatemalan accent and odd syntax. He started his career selling tortillas door to door. After many 75-hour weeks, he now owns a supermarket in Raleigh, where a mostly-immigrant clientele pays cash for Latin pop music, live tilapia [fish] and a wide variety of chillies. Mr Roldan is proud of his hard-earned wealth, but not as proud as he is of his daughter's MBA from Stanford.

Making the Most of Opportunity

Immigrants' children are typically American citizens, having been born on American soil. More than 90% speak English fluently; by the third generation, 72% speak nothing else. Many help their less-fluent parents with form-filling, as other children help their elders navigate the internet. The parents, in turn, try to infuse their offspring with their work ethic and entrepreneurial spirit. (Latinos open new firms at a rate three times the national norm.)

Miguel Lopez, who arrived from Mexico when he was 17, says his children will have a double advantage over him. Not only are they native-born Americans, but they are "native-born" to the information age. Mr Lopez is not doing badly himself: he owns a small window-cleaning firm. He woos customers by giving them instant estimates, which he can do because he looks at satellite photos of their houses online. His firm grossed $150,000 [in 2005]. With only a high-school education, he says, there is no other country where he could live so well. But his children will go to college, he says, and do something better than washing windows.

Conditions Depicted in
The Jungle Are Returning

Eric Schlosser

Eric Schlosser is a writer known for his investigative and muck-raking journalism and has often been compared with Upton Sinclair. He is the author of Fast Food Nation, *an exposé on the fast-food industry.*

Despite the success of The Jungle, *the book helped change food preparation conditions in the United States more than it affected worker's rights. Nevertheless, in the years after the publication of* The Jungle, *working conditions at meatpacking plants steadily improved, largely as a result of labor unions. But with the rise of the fast-food industry in the 1960s and 1970s, many of the same abuses Sinclair chronicled began to return to the meatpacking industry. Today, workers' rights are routinely infringed upon by powerful corporations, and food safety is again a major concern.*

One hundred years ago American business leaders and politicians celebrated the free market. They praised the virtues of small government, competition, and laissez-faire [the principle of no regulation of industry] capitalism. They said that with enough hard work anybody could make it to the top. Although free market rhetoric was plentiful in those days, free markets were hard to find. Almost every sector of the American economy was controlled by a handful of corporations whose executives met in secret, set prices, determined wages, and conspired to destroy labor unions. These interlocking corporate and financial monopolies had a pleasant, innocent-sounding name: trusts. There was a steel trust, a sugar trust, and a coal trust, among others. The markets weren't free, but the trusts were—free to employ children in factories, free to make people work sixty or seventy hours a week, free to pollute rivers and streams, to hire private armies, to bribe state legislators and members of Congress, to sell what they wanted at whatever price they liked.

Blind Greed

The freedom of big business seemed limitless. Drug companies sold patent medicines containing heroin, morphine, and cocaine that promised to cure all sorts of diseases, but actually cured none of them. Food companies sold children's candy colored with toxic heavy metals. Cheap margarine was routinely marketed as butter. Crude mixtures of apple scraps, glucose, timothy seeds, and food coloring made from coal tar were sold as strawberry jam. In the age of the great trusts, the gulf between the wealthy and the poor became enormous. Robber barons built their homes in imitation of European palaces, while millions of American workers lived in urban slums.

Upton Sinclair was moved by these injustices. During the fall of 1904 he left his home in New Jersey and traveled to Chicago, intending to write a novel about the plight of the city's meatpacking workers. The beef trust controlled the industry with an iron fist. It had recently crushed a strike by union members who were seeking a pay raise of less than three cents an hour. The meatpacking industry seemed to embody everything that was wrong with American society, operating largely in secret, wielding unchecked power, threatening the health of workers and consumers. As Sinclair later argued in *The Jungle*, the beef trust was "the incarnation of blind and insensate greed . . . the Great Butcher . . . the spirit of capitalism made flesh."

Dedicated to the Workingmen of America

Sinclair was a socialist with grand ambitions. He set out to write a book that would do for workers what *Uncle Tom's*

Cabin had done for slaves half a century earlier. *Uncle Tom's Cabin* was considered the most important novel ever published in the United States. It had played a central role in creating public outrage toward slavery and widespread support for a war to liberate the slaves. Sinclair was aiming pretty high. He was only twenty-six years old, and his previous novel had sold fewer than two thousand copies. He spent seven weeks in Chicago, wandering through the stockyards and slaughter-houses, visiting the homes of meatpacking workers, listening to their stories and filling his notebooks with the details of their lives. Living on advances from a socialist newspaper, the *Appeal to Reason*, and a New York publisher, Macmillan, he returned to New Jersey and started writing on Christmas morning 1904.

The Jungle tells the story of a Lithuanian immigrant, Jurgis Rudkus, his family, and his friends. It describes the terrible working conditions in meatpacking plants, the squalid housing, the ruthlessness of employers, the sexual harassment, the lure of alcoholism and prostitution, the political corruption, the misery of life in jail. It depicts a world where honest, decent people are transformed into cogs in a huge industrial machine. It upends the traditional rags-to-riches success story, portraying a downward spiral. The immigrants are exploited and discarded, not rewarded and applauded for their hard work. At a time when most popular fiction dealt with the problems of the middle or upper class, Sinclair focused on life at the bottom. He dedicated *The Jungle* "To the Workingmen of America."

Unexpected Response

Published as weekly installments in the *Appeal to Reason*, the novel was popular among socialists. When it appeared as a book in February 1906—published by Doubleday, Page after Macmillan rejected it for being too graphic—*The Jungle* quickly became an international bestseller. Foreign critics such as Winston Churchill, praised the book's critique of unchecked greed in the United States. American readers, however, responded in a way that Sinclair had not expected. They were outraged by his account of unsanitary conditions in the nation's slaughterhouses. Sausage made from rancid meat laced with chemicals to disguise the smell; sausage made out of dead rats; beef hearts and other organ meats artificially colored and sold as canned chicken; goat meat sold as lamb; a worker accidentally killed and boiled and turned into lard—although these descriptions filled a small fraction of the book, they dominated the media frenzy surrounding its publication. Within weeks, Upton Sinclair was transformed from an obscure young writer into an internationally renowned novelist.

One of the most remarkable aspects of American political life a century ago is that the White House was occupied by a Republican pro-business president who loved to read books—even books by socialists like Leo Tolstoy and Upton Sinclair. President Theodore Roosevelt not only read *The Jungle*, but thought that much of what it described seemed accurate. He was wary of the concentrated economic power that the trusts represented and felt that the beef trust, in particular, was capable of unscrupulous behavior. While serving as an officer during the Spanish-American War, he'd been appalled by the poor quality of the canned meats sold to the War Department and served to his troops in Cuba. It was widely believed that such "embalmed beef" had killed more American soldiers than Spanish bullets did. Roosevelt invited Upton Sinclair to the White House, met with him, and didn't like him. He thought that Sinclair was too hypersensitive and high-strung. Nevertheless, he promised to investigate the accusations made in *The Jungle* and take action if they proved to be true.

Teddy Roosevelt's Response

At Roosevelt's request, two separate investigations were conducted. The first, led by officials at the U.S. Department of

Agriculture (USDA), concluded that Sinclair was responsible for "willful and deliberate misrepresentation of fact" and had exaggerated the problems in the meatpacking industry. Suspicious of the USDA's close ties to the beef trust, Roosevelt secretly asked a pair of trusted advisors, Charles P. Neill, the U.S. Commisioner of Labor, and James B. Reynolds, a New York social worker, to visit slaughterhouses in Chicago and assess the accuracy of Sinclair's claims. Reynolds and Neill witnessed sanitary conditions that were far from ideal. "In a word," the two reported, "we saw meat shoveled from filthy wooden floors, piled on tables rarely washed, pushed from room to room in rotten box carts, in all of which processes it was in the way of gathering dirt, splinters, floor filth, and the expectorations of tuberculous and other diseased workers." They saw workers urinating on the floor near the meat. They saw canned meat that was two years old being relabeled and sold as new. Their report convinced Roosevelt that Upton Sinclair was right.

President Roosevelt used the controversy and public outrage inspired by *The Jungle* to seek passage of two important pieces of legislation: the Pure Food and Drug Act and the Meat Inspection Act. Both promised an unprecedented expansion of federal power, allowing the government to regulate the safety and purity of food transported across state lines. Both were vehemently opposed by the beef trust and big business. The meatpacking industry attacked Roosevelt and Sinclair, arguing that the federal government should not infringe upon states' rights or interfere with the free market. The states' rights argument was especially appealing to the trusts, since state legislators were much less expensive to bribe than members of Congress. A handful of companies supported Roosevelt's legislation. In their view the absence of government regulation punished firms that tried to behave responsibly and helped those that cut corners, misled consumers, and sold dangerous goods.

New Laws

In June 1906, four months after the publication of *The Jungle*, the Pure Food and Drug Act and the Meat Inspection Act were passed by Congress. Although industry pressure had watered down some of their provisions, these two bills marked a turning point in the role of the federal government. For the next seventy-five years, the police power guaranteed by the U.S. Constitution was used to protect ordinary consumers from corporate misbehavior. The federal government assumed the responsibility for ensuring food safety, automobile safety, clean water, clear air. The results were far from perfect, but a new template had been created, one that declared the public interest to be more important than the demands of private interests. Upton Sinclair was disappointed, however, by the impact of *The Jungle*. It had been written to help meatpacking workers, not to improve the quality of meat. "I aimed for the public's heart," Sinclair later wrote, "and by accident hit it in the stomach."

Gradual Improvement in Working Conditions

So what happened to American meatpacking workers in the years following *The Jungle*? The conditions in slaughterhouses gradually improved—not because of Upton Sinclair and not because of any sudden burst of corporate social responsibility. Things got better because labor unions fought to make them better. It took years of patient organizing and a great deal of struggle. The meatpacking companies did all they could to thwart unions, pitting one ethnic group against another, encouraging rivalries between Irish immigrants and Lithuanians, between Poles and Slovaks, between whites and African Americans. By the late 1930s, however, most of the industry was unionized. And by the mid-1950s, meatpacking workers had one of the highest-paid manufacturing jobs in the United

States. It was still a dirty and dangerous job. But it had finally become a good job, with decent wages, health benefits, and pension plans. It provided a solid middle-class income. There were waiting lists for jobs at American slaughterhouses. By 1970, the typical meatpacking worker enjoyed an income 20 percent higher than the typical factory worker. And the beef trust was gone, relegated to the history books, just a bad memory from a distant era. In 1917 President Woodrow Wilson had launched a major assault on the beef trust, and after decades of federal antitrust enforcement there was a truly competitive market. Hundreds of small companies thrived, and by 1970 the four largest beef firms controlled only 20 percent of the market.

Social Problems Alleviated

The social problems outlined in *The Jungle* had largely been solved. Fundamental changes in the meatpacking industry seemed to confirm the validity of the American dream. Children enjoyed a higher standard of living than their parents, and poor immigrants comfortably became part of the mainstream. Then the tide began to turn. During the 1970s fast food chains like McDonald's began to play a larger role in the market, purchasing large volumes of frozen ground beef. Their demand for a uniform product that would taste the same at thousands of locations encouraged the rise of big meat suppliers. A new meatpacking company, IBP, opened slaughterhouses in rural areas where labor unions were weak. IBP battled unions, cut wages by as much as 5.0 percent, and recruited immigrants from Mexico. The election of Ronald Reagan to the presidency in 1980 revived the faith in free markets, small government, and laissez faire. Antitrust enforcement was discouraged, big meatpacking companies swallowed the little ones, and gains that had taken decades to achieve vanished within a few years.

Cutting Workers' Rights

Today the American beef industry is more centralized and more concentrated than it was when *The Jungle* first appeared. At the height of the beef trust, the five largest companies controlled 55 percent of the market. Today the four largest beef companies control more than 80 percent of the market. One of those firms, Tyson Foods, is now the largest meatpacking company the world has ever seen. After purchasing IBP, it became the leading processor of beef as well as poultry. Every week, Tyson slaughters five million chickens, almost half a million hogs, and a quarter of a million cattle. The industrialization of meatpacking that Upton Sinclair depicts in *The Jungle* has been taken to new heights. And the effort to exploit and intimidate poor immigrant workers has resumed. In recent years, Tyson Foods has led the way in cutting wages, reducing benefits, and breaking labor unions. As the industry leader, it sets the standard that other companies must follow. As a result, there are no waiting lists for employment at American slaughterhouses today. The typical meatpacking worker now earns wages that are 24 percent lower than that of the typical factory worker.

Despite all the technological advances over the past century, much of the work in a modern slaughterhouse would be familiar to Upton Sinclair. The most important tool is still a sharp knife. Hundreds of workers now stand along a single production line, wielding knives. When the line moves too quickly, people get hurt. The most common injury is a laceration, as workers stab themselves or someone nearby. Management tactics described in *The Jungle* have become commonplace again: the relentless pressure to speed up production, to minimize the severity of injuries, to get rid of workers who can no longer keep up the pace. Today roughly 80 percent of the nation's meatpacking workers are Latino. Most of them cannot speak English, and many are illegal immigrants. Like the Eastern European immigrants that Sinclair depicted, they are vulnerable, fearful, and unlikely to complain. They have one of the most dangerous jobs in the United States. Thanks to the influence of the big meatpacking companies, the federal government no longer shows much interest in preventing—or even counting—the serious injuries that occur every day.

New Food Contamination Issues

During the same years that the working conditions got worse in the meatpacking industry, so did the threat of contamination. The centralization of the industry has made it easier for harmful pathogens to cause widespread outbreaks of food-borne illness. A generation ago, contaminated meat at a butcher shop or a small processing plant might sicken people in the local community. Today just thirteen slaughterhouses process most of the beef consumed in the United States. Food safety problems at a single slaughterhouse can cause outbreaks that extend not only nationwide, but worldwide. The USDA, which is responsible for the safety of meat, has been largely captured by the industry it is supposed to regulate. At a time when dangerous new pathogens like *E. coli* O157:H7 are emerging, food safety regulations have been weakened and companies have been given greater freedom to monitor their own practices. Although rats are no longer being turned into sausage, unappetizing things still wind up in meat. The fecal contamination of ground beef explains why ordering a hamburger medium rare now qualifies as a form of high-risk behavior. A single bite of a tainted burger can make you extremely ill.

Back in the Jungle

The United States in the first decade of the twenty-first century bears an unfortunate resemblance to that of a century ago. Once again free market rhetoric cloaks an absence of free markets, a handful of companies control the leading sectors of the economy, the political system is corrupted by money, and the gulf between rich and poor is widening. Once again the meatpacking industry serves as an excellent symbol of all these larger social trends. Upton Sinclair's youthful ambition to write a novel that would match the influence of *Uncle Tom's Cabin* no longer seems arrogant or delusional. *The Jungle* has never been out of print and is still widely read throughout the world. It captures something essential about the American immigrant experience and the workings of a brutal industrial system. It transcends the specifics of one historical era and sadly remains relevant to our own. At this very moment, some contemporary version of Jurgis Rudkus is illegally crossing the border between Mexico and Arizona with dreams of a better life.

The socialism that Upton Sinclair advocated never took hold in the United States. Most likely it would've been a disaster. The utopia described at the end of *The Jungle*—featuring "the most improved machinery employed, under the direction of expert agricultural chemists"—brings to mind the worst of modern American agribusiness and Soviet central planning. Theodore Roosevelt admired *The Jungle*, but had one major complaint about the book: "I wish he had left out the ridiculous socialist rant at the end of it." Most literary critics would agree, and even Upton Sinclair later admitted to feeling that way. Having spent months furiously writing the book, he was exhausted and unable to think of a good way to conclude it. No novelist should be expected to provide neat solutions to extraordinarily complex problems. Upton Sinclair's achievement was impressive enough. He saw through the lies of his era and exposed a world long hidden from view. He showed compassion for the weak and the poor, the powerless and the despised. He created images and characters that are poignant and memorable. He fueled anger at injustice. It is no fault of his that the old lies have lately been repeated, that important lessons have been forgotten, and that somehow we now find ourselves back in the jungle, with an odd feeling of déjà vu.

Social Issues
in Literature

CHAPTER 3

Contemporary Perspectives on Workers' Rights

The United States Must
Support Its Poorest Workers

Beth Shulman

Beth Shulman is a lawyer and a consultant on work-related is-
sues. She is the author of The Betrayal of Work: How Low-
Wage Jobs Fail 30 Million Americans and Their Families.

Despite the common American belief that all those who work
hard should be able to provide for their families, many low-
income wage earners live in poverty. As the middle income
bracket diminishes due to a decline in the manufacturing sector,
America is divided into two groups: highly educated, high-
earning professionals and blue-collar, low-income earners. In or-
der to ensure that the latter group can live the American dream,
three steps need to be taken. First, the United States needs an
adequate minimum wage; second, businesses that support their
workers should be rewarded; and third, strong unions need to
fight for workers' rights. The working poor place a great burden
on the United States. Government programs fill vital gaps in
health care and other services when private enterprise will not
provide workers a minimal standard of living. America must act
on these measures for its own good.

Americans share a tacit understanding—a belief, a promise—that everyone who works hard will be able to
provide for themselves and their families. But for more than
30 million Americans in low-wage jobs, that promise has been
broken. One in four workers does not make enough to secure
the basic necessities of life.

Beth Shulman, "Making Work Pay," *Ending Poverty in America: How to Restore the*
American Dream, New York: The New Press, 2007, pp. 114–124. Compilation copyright © 2007 by the University of North Carolina at Chapel Hill on behalf of the Center
on Poverty, Work and Opportunity. Essay copyright © Beth Shulman. Reproduced by
permission of The New Press, www.thenewpress.com, (800) 233-4830.

An Hourglass Economy

How do we fulfill the promise that honest labor will ensure a decent life? How do we create family-sustaining jobs? How do we make work pay? The American economy today [in 2007] looks more and more like an hourglass, with most of the jobs created in the last two decades clustered at the high and low ends of the income scale. At the high end are managerial and professional jobs that require at least a four-year college degree. At the low end are jobs such as home health aides, janitors, security guards, hotel workers, nursing-home workers, and food workers that pay little more than the minimum wage.

In the middle, and now conspicuous by their absence, used to be millions of manufacturing and technical jobs that practically guaranteed a hardworking American a good wage, decent health insurance, vacation time, and even a pension. The U.S. Congressional Budget Office estimates that the manufacturing sector alone has lost more than three million jobs between July 2000 and January 2004.

A critical fact is that there is nothing inherent in putting together cars or handling molten steel that made these jobs "good." In fact, at one time these jobs were hazardous, low-wage jobs that provided few benefits. But they became the good jobs of the twentieth century because we as Americans made them that way. Through unionization and social legislation we pressured companies to provide good salaries and benefits to workers in the manufacturing industries.

In exactly the same way, nothing is inherently bad about the job of a childcare worker, nursing-home aide, security guard, emergency medical technician, janitor, or hotel worker. It is time we discarded the notion that something intrinsic in a particular job chains it forever to low pay and miserable conditions. It is not what one does on the job that determines whether it is a "good" or "bad" job. Employers make decisions about the working conditions of that job, and we as a nation can influence those decisions.

Today's low-wage service jobs can easily become the good jobs of the twenty-first century. The best part: these jobs cannot be shipped overseas. Unlike the task of putting a car or a computer together, these jobs must be done here in the United States where the consumers live. Workers living in China or Bangalore simply cannot be our security guards, nursing-home aides, or restaurant workers. And these jobs are continuing to grow. According to the Bureau of Labor Statistics, 5 out of every 10 new positions will be in these low-wage service jobs.

Today the question is whether the people who protect our families, clean our office building, process our food, care for our children, and comfort our aged loved ones will have the resources to provide for their own families. A few simple steps could ensure that America's economic growth and profitability translate into a better life for all working Americans.

An Adequate Minimum Wage

Modernizing the minimum wage is the first step toward ensuring that work provides the basics of a decent life. Our nation established a federal minimum wage in 1938 because we believed in the basic human dignity of work: no job should pay so little that it impoverishes Americans. But the fixed-level approach to the minimum wage fails dismally to keep up with the cost of living. The federal minimum wage has been frozen at $5.15 an hour since 1997, and its buying power in 2006 was at its lowest level since 1955. As this volume goes to press [in 2007], the Democratically-controlled 110th Congress is seeking to increase the minimum wage to $7.25 an hour[1] One way to measure the worth of the minimum wage is against the average hourly wage. In the 1950s and 1960s the minimum wage averaged half of average hourly earnings. In 2006 the mini-

1. The minimum wage was raised to just $5.85 by Congress in July 2007.

mum was only 31 percent of average hourly earnings, its lowest level in more than 50 years. That translated into barely more than $10,000 a year for full-time workers, around half the federal poverty level for a family of four.

Raising the minimum wage to what it would have been if it had merely kept up with inflation from its peak in purchasing power in 1968 (a little over $9.00 an hour according to the U.S. Bureau of Labor Statistics Inflation Calculator) and indexing it to the inflation rate to preserve those gains is a good first step to ensuring that work pays. The change would not bring minimum-wage workers into the middle class nor make up for the years of lost income, but it would at least bring them back to what they would have made had their wages kept up with inflation. It would also respond to the escalating costs of housing, health care, transportation, and college Americans are facing. And numerous studies have found that any change in the minimum wage has a ripple effect, helping workers who make more as well. Raising the wage floor would also help stop employers from restructuring jobs by cutting workers' wages and farming out the work to even lower-wage employers.

Opponents' Arguments

Opponents of the minimum-wage increase argue that a raise will not lift the earnings of the lowest-wage workers because it is not well targeted to them. Yet the poorest 40 percent of households are those that reap the most gains from any wage increase, according to the Economic Policy Institute, and that includes seven million children under 12 who live in households with minimum-wage earners. And contrary to popular myth that most minimum-wage workers are teenagers, 80 percent of the recipients of a raise are adults. Women, who represent 60 percent of minimum-wage workers, would disproportionately benefit. Studies show that a raise in the minimum wage does in fact decrease poverty.

Another canard against minimum-wage raises is that businesses will respond by slashing the number of jobs they offer. History does not bear this out. Recent studies by the Economic Policy Institute found no statistically significant job losses resulting from the last federal minimum-wage increase, in 1996–97. Other studies of the 1990–91 federal minimum-wage increase had similar findings, as did studies of various state minimum-wage increases. . . .

It is clear, in short, that raising the minimum wage has many economic benefits that reach beyond the workers who would directly benefit. Americans at the state level understand this. Frustrated by Congress's inability to move, 29 states, including more than half the national workforce, have increased their minimum-wage levels above the federal minimum through legislative action or state ballot initiatives. Many of these states also increase their wages to reflect inflation. And more states are expected to raise their minimum wage as well. This revolution is not surprising. Recent polling shows that 80 percent of Americans support an increase in the minimum wage. Even Nevada and Florida, two states that went for George W. Bush in the 2000 election, voted to hike the state minimum wage past the federal level.

The minimum wage is not a liberal or conservative issue. It is a human issue. Modernizing it by restoring its value and indexing it is a crucial step in addressing the problem of inadequate wages and inadequate rewards for a hard day's work—but it is only the first step.

Rewarding Businesses That Treat Workers Fairly

Living-wage ordinances provide incentives for employers to provide good jobs. A living-wage ordinance applies to entities that do business with or get benefits from a city, state, or the federal government in the form of subsidies, contracts, or tax abatements or in other ways. It requires such companies to

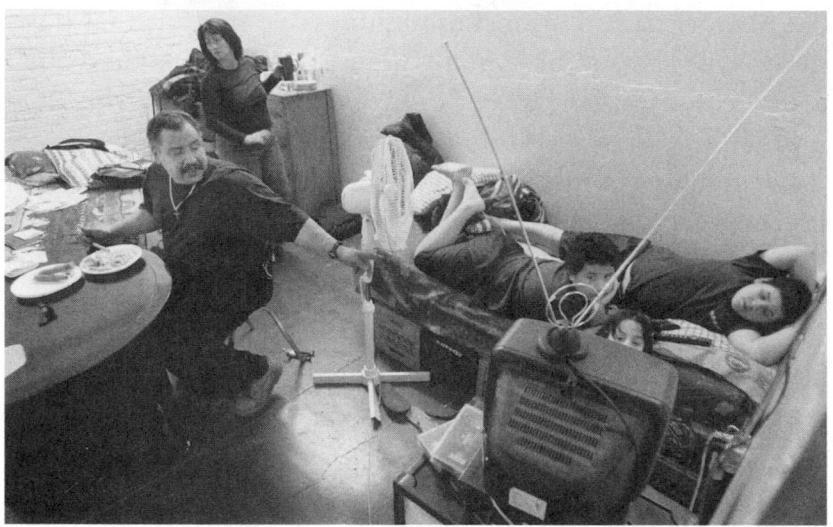

Jesus Torres and his family relax after work, in their room at a Chicago homeless shelter. Some feel that the laws should be changed to boost pay and help bring families like this one out of poverty. AP Images.

provide a certain living wage and certain basic benefits to their workers. The premise is that corporations that receive taxpayers' dollars should not be using that money to impoverish those taxpayers.

To date there are more than 130 living-wage ordinances around the United States. The first was enacted in Baltimore in 1994. All the laws differ in what employers must provide, but the common element is a requirement for a wage level that allows workers to provide the basics of a decent life for themselves and their families. Some ordinances also require that employers provide health benefits or stay neutral in union organizing campaigns. Behind all of them is a commitment to creating family-sustaining jobs.

The concept of a living wage is different from that of the minimum wage. A minimum wage is a floor beyond which our society believes an employer should not go. A living wage considers what it really takes to make a family self-sufficient— that is, to obtain the basic necessities without government assistance. A living-wage calculation also considers the relative prices in particular geographic areas.

Although the official poverty line is supposed to define an adequate income, many leading scholars agree that the current measure is wholly inadequate and outdated. The official poverty measure assumes erroneously, for example, that food costs about one-third of a family's budget and that everything else takes up the remainder. Calculators therefore merely multiply the price of a "typical" family food basket by three and call the result the official poverty line. Today, however, food costs less than 20 percent of an average household's budget. Housing, health care, and work expenses such as child care and transportation are usually a family's biggest costs. The official poverty line is therefore considered to be only about 60 percent of what it really takes to make ends meet.

The impact of the living-wage movement goes beyond the number of ordinances that have been enacted. Mostly local, they cover a relatively small number of people working at businesses that have certain kinds of contracts with local governments. Yet the concept of requiring companies to pay a living wage and provide basic benefits if they do business with the government has widened.

It is used in economic development at both the state and local levels. In 2003 Good Jobs First, a national policy resource center for corporate and government accountability in economic development, found that at least 89 jurisdictions, including 43 states, 41 cities, and 5 counties, had attached job quality standards to at least one development subsidy. Since that time the number has significantly increased. More recently the community benefits movement has been reframing the debate on economic development, creating agreements not only on minimum job standards but on housing and neighborhood services for public-private development projects.

Cities are starting to require certain kinds of businesses to pay a living wage if they want to do business in their city. In

Emeryville, outside San Francisco, a local law requires hotels to pay workers overall wages of $11 per hour. Through this growing push for living-wage provisions, the notion of a living wage has begun to take hold as an important goal in our society. The more it is used, the more it will begin to set norms about acceptable pay for workers in a given area. If it were used more widely throughout government, the concept could have a significant impact on overall wage levels and other elements of decent jobs. . . .

Living-wage ordinances could counteract the current harmful trend of a "race to the bottom," where local jurisdictions try to attract employers by offering larger subsidies than their neighbors. The more widespread living-wage ordinances are, the less able businesses will be to shop around for the cheapest workforce. Living-wage ordinances are one tool to ensure that economic development policies create good jobs.

Critics of living-wage ordinances have only one argument, and it is a false one: they assert that government should not intervene in the free marketplace. But governments intervene in the market all the time, primarily to help businesses—through such measures as crop and export subsidies, tax breaks, special exemptions, regulatory changes, and earmarked government projects. Living-wage laws merely set some socially important conditions for receiving those benefits, conditions that help the entire community by providing good jobs.

Facilitating Strong Unions

So how can we enact adequate minimum-wage and living-wage laws and ensure that employers adequately reward workers? One answer is to facilitate unionization. It has often been said that the best antipoverty program is a strong union. At the height of union representation in the mid-twentieth century, when 35 percent of the American labor force was organized, wages rose significantly nationwide. Millions of people moved into the middle class, creating what would be the most equal distribution of income this country has ever seen. Union contracts provided health-care coverage, paid vacations, and pension benefits to millions, and union political clout helped win passage of Social Security, Medicare, and Medicaid—the country's social safety net.

Today, however, with union representation down to 7.8 percent of the private-sector economy, America suffers from the greatest income inequality since the Gilded Age. Amid increased worker productivity and skyrocketing corporate profits, ordinary Americans' wages have stagnated, not even keeping pace with inflation. Employers continue to shift more and more of the daily risks of working life onto their employees, so that more and more working families must rely on unstable jobs without health insurance, retirement security, or paid time off. Working conditions have deteriorated, so that many jobholders must work off the clock, in unsafe conditions, or under enormous stress.

Can unions do anything about this situation? Should we care that union representation is so low? The answer is most definitely yes.

No one can deny that unions have increased the paychecks of the workers who are organized under a collective bargaining agreement. According to the Economic Policy Institute, unions raise the wages of unionized workers by roughly 20 percent over those of their nonunionized counterparts. In traditionally low-wage service jobs such as hotel maintenance, nursing-home care, home health care, security services, and manual labor, unionized workers make 27 percent more. Because unions have a greater impact on low- and middle-income jobs than on high-wage positions, they reduce wage inequality.

But wages are not the only difference. Fully 86 percent of union workers are covered by health benefits through their employer, according to the Employee Benefit Research Institute, compared with 59 percent of nonunion workers. Union-

157

ized workers are also 54 percent more likely to have employer-provided pension plans, and they receive 26 percent more vacation time.

Unions also bring workers a voice and basic dignity on their jobs. As a nonunion Alabama nursing-home worker stated, "You tell the supervisors that a resident in the nursing home isn't breathing right and they don't do anything. They have a suggestion box. But they never take your advice. I have suggestions regarding the residents because I'm with them all the time, but they never listen. That's why I want a union.". . .

When unions have a presence in an industry, they set norms that put pressure on nonunion employers in that industry to improve their wages and benefits. Again in Los Angeles, after . . . security guards were unionized at several companies, nonunion employers raised their wages from $7.64 to $8.50 an hour in order to compete for workers and to stave off the unions. Nonunion workers benefit from strong unions that can set a pay and benefit standard. A high-school graduate whose workplace is not unionized, for example, but whose industry is 25 percent unionized is paid 5 percent more than similar workers in less unionized industries. . . .

Unions historically led the fight for the average American. Remember the bumper sticker "Unions—the folks who brought you the weekend"? As columnist David Broder aptly stated, "When labor lobbied powerfully on Capitol Hill, it did not confine itself to bread-and-butter issues for its own members. It was at the forefront of battles for aid to education, civil rights, housing programs and a host of other social causes important to the whole community. And because it was muscular, it was heard and heeded." It is no coincidence, then, that the decline of the labor movement has been accompanied by rising inequality, a dramatic decline in the value of the minimum wage, bankruptcy reform that chiefly hurt ordinary

Americans, and tax cuts for the wealthy, while at the same time social programs that help ordinary Americans come under the knife.

So why aren't more workers organizing in American workplaces? Polls show that they would like to: 53 million Americans said in a recent Peter D. Hart Research Associates poll that they would support having a union at their job site if they were given the chance. That is the problem: they are not getting that chance.

The National Labor Relations Act guarantees workers the right to form and join unions for the purpose of collective bargaining, Yet today's workers have virtually lost the right to organize. Virulent antilabor campaigns are common when workers attempt to organize, and current labor laws are both weak and poorly enforced. They do very little to deter illegal anti-union behavior, and complaints to the National Labor Relations Board (NLRB) often take years to resolve.

Anti-Union Activities

In a return to the bad old days, American workers who try to organize unions face employer harassment, intimidation, or worse. According to a 2000 Human Rights Watch report, "Workers who try to form and join trade unions to bargain with their employers are spied on, harassed, pressured, threatened, suspended, fired, deported, or otherwise victimized in reprisal for their exercise of the right to freedom of association."

These acts of illegal employer intimidation have accelerated in recent years. In the 1950s the annual number of workers who suffered reprisals for trying to organize a union was in the hundreds. By 1990 it had climbed to 20,000. That horrific number continues to grow. The Center for Urban Economic Development found in a 2005 study that when faced with organizing drives, 30 percent of employers fire pro-union workers, 49 percent threaten to close a worksite if the union prevails, and 51 percent coerce workers into opposing unions with bribery or favoritism. . . .

America needs to reform its labor laws to make it very costly for corporations to take the low road of violating their workers' human rights to organize a union. And then we must enforce those laws and treat those abusive companies as law-breakers, for that is what they are. If we want to create family-sustaining jobs and improve wages, benefits, and working conditions for everyday Americans, workers must have a free and unfettered choice to form and join a union in an environment that is free of any kind of employer intimidation.

America Must Act

Every day in America, low-wage workers make our lives possible through their labor as security guards and teaching assistants, nursing-home aides and hospital workers, janitors and hotel workers, child-care workers and retail clerks. Yet we have turned these hardworking men and women and their families into the new poor. It is a blight on our democracy and our understanding of fair play that in such a prosperous country hardworking Americans cannot make ends meet no matter how hard they work.

It also has social costs. We all pay when wages do not support families. Taxpayers pay when they have to pick up the bill for employers whose wages do not cover housing, health care, or food. Communities pay as their tax base dwindles and the social ills of deprivation spread through their towns. Society pays as we become more economically polarized. As human beings, we all pay when we turn our backs on our fellow Americans who are working just as hard as we are but still cannot provide for their families.

It is clear that companies can remain competitive in the global economy by paying a living wage and providing basic benefits. But Americans should not leave it up to corporations to make the decision about how their workers are treated.

That is our role as a society. It is up to us to ensure that work pays. We can make choices that ensure that work provides the basics of a decent life and that hardworking men and women and their families have a shot at the American Dream. All we have to do is act.

Labor Unions Must Meet Workers' Needs in a Changing World

James O'Toole and Edward E. Lawler III

James O'Toole is the principal author of the federal government's "Work in America" report. He is the author of more than a dozen books on management and leadership. Edward E. Lawler III has served as director of the Center for Effective Organizations and has taught at the Marshall School of Business at the University of Southern California. He has authored or coedited more than forty books.

Since 1978, union membership has declined significantly. Reasons for this decline include: the failure of unions to participate in the quality of work life movement; an unwillingness to address broader issues of business effectiveness and performance; an inability to cooperate with business management; and the rise of alternative voices for workers, including legal representation. In general, unions failed to change as an isolated and domestic American economy became more interconnected and global. Although unions are not as strong as they once were, their usefulness in protecting workers' rights remains. American workers continue to support organized representation in principle, if not in numbers, and unions must improve their "products" if they wish to gain back lost laborers.

In the 1970s, the trade union movement provided a voice for the American workforce. Through collective bargaining, unions won wage and benefit premiums for their members and provided a vehicle for them to pursue grievances against employers with regard to working conditions and the nature of supervision. Approximately 25 percent of the U.S. workforce belonged to unions in 1973, and many more were positively affected by the contracts unions negotiated and the political actions they undertook on their behalf. Indeed, powerful unions were an omnipresent influence, affecting the votes of legislators and the practices of almost all employers. The mere threat of being unionized caused many nonorganized companies to raise the pay of their workers and to put grievance procedures into place.

The Decline in Union Membership

A major decline in union membership began in the early 1980s and has continued ever since. By 2004, only 12 percent of the U.S. workforce was organized. The decline has been particularly steep in the private sector, where less than 8 percent of workers are now in unions. While the public sector remains a labor stronghold, with 36.4 percent of government workers unionized, even there union membership is decreasing as a percentage of the total public-sector employment. A number of factors have contributed to the dramatic drop in union membership, most notably the decline in the manufacturing sector, which had historically been the base of union membership in the United States. For example, as the result of a sharp decrease in the number of production workers employed by American car manufacturers, membership in the United Auto Workers (UAW) has dropped from a high of over 1.5 million thirty years ago to less than half a million today [in 2006]. The automobile industry also provides a clear illustration of the second major factor in the decline of the union movement: the inability to organize new facilities and companies. The UAW has not succeeded in organizing workers in U.S. auto plants owned by Toyota, Honda, and Nissan. In addition, most of the fastest-growing domestic industries in recent decades have remained nonunion: Silicon Valley, for example, is virtually without unions.

The *Work in America* report identified a third reason for the decline of the union Movement. Inexplicably, union leaders did not play a significant role in the efforts from 1970 to 1990 to improve the quality of work life in America. Although the report cited a few sterling examples of successful union/management joint efforts to foster employee involvement and to redesign jobs to make them more satisfying, by and large, unions took a pass on what proved to be the most significant workplace reform movement of the last half of the twentieth century. And unions largely have stayed on the sidelines during the growth of employee stock ownership.

Reasons for Union Decline

The failure of unions to participate in the quality of work life (QWL) movement, let alone their refusal to lead it, has undercut their power and credibility. Many of the "green-field" High-Involvement factories built in the 1970s and 1980s—such as the pathbreaking General Foods plant in Topeka, Kansas—have been able to remain nonunion precisely because most employees have felt that their jobs would get worse if they joined a union. In the team environment at the General Foods plant, employees had greater autonomy, freedom, and opportunity to learn than did workers in a typical union plant. When interviewed about their own interest in union membership, many replied that a union would not provide the kind of "voice" that they wanted. In fact, many felt it would take away from their ability to influence managerial decisions.

The failure of unions to support efforts to improve the quality of work life coincided with, or perhaps was the result of, their unwillingness to speak out on the broader issues of business effectiveness and performance. When foreign competition threatened the survival of American manufacturers, unions chose to continue to voice traditional employee demands for higher wages, better benefits, and safer working conditions. By and large they succeeded in those areas, but they failed to provide an effective response to the challenges of globalization. To be fair, the American trade union movement suffers from a major disadvantage in dealing with the effects of globalization: unions are local, but an increasing number of major corporations are global. Thus, when faced with tough union demands, employers increasingly move jobs to other countries. Unions do not have the option of following the companies, nor can they negotiate globally since, in most cases, they are purely domestic organizations.

Nonetheless, union practices and policies contributed, to at least some degree, to the decline of many U.S. rustbelt industries—steel, chemicals, and autos. The promising union/management cooperation programs started in the 1970s originally had been intended to give unions a voice in improving manufacturing company operations on the theory that workers can't thrive unless their employers survive. The hope at the time was that unions would come to see that the issue wasn't simply what companies could do for union members but also what workers could do for their employers, so that the company then would be able to do more for them in the long run. But union leaders did not see cooperation with management as a part of their role, and they walked away from the programs. The most recent casualty in this regard was the cooperative effort by General Motors [GM] and the UAW to create "a different kind of car company" at GM's Saturn division. After years of backtracking by both the company and the union, in 2005 Saturn was finally and fully reabsorbed as just another part of GM, subjecting the division's employees both to conventional working conditions and to adversarial labor-management relations.

Another reason why unions have declined is the advent of alternative voices for workers, starting with the fact that many employers at long last have learned to listen to their people. As corporations have increasingly recognized that their employees are not only keys to the success of their operations but, in fact, real and valuable assets, managers have become more willing to pay attention to worker needs, wants, ideas, and suggestions than they were thirty years ago. Today almost all major corporations conduct annual employee surveys to gather information about attitudes and morale. And the most progressive employers have learned that if they give their employees what unions provide—good salaries and benefits, safe working conditions, and a grievance procedure—most will not want a union.

Lawyers also have become voices for employees. Many issues that used to be handled by grievance procedures now end up in the hands of lawyers who file individual or class action suits on behalf of employees who claim they have been unfairly paid, dismissed, or harassed. Because the settlements lawyers win often are larger than those won in traditional grievance procedures, to some degree lawyers have become an effective substitute for unions. Finally, the loudest voice for employees on many issues is the federal and state legislation that now covers many of the practices for which unions once bargained.

Failure to Respond to Change

In most other developed countries, it is much easier for unions to organize plants, offices, and stores than in the United States, where courts and legislatures have made it difficult for unions to expand their membership. While there is no doubt that American employers have succeeded in their legal and political efforts to make union organization difficult, the trade union movement mainly has itself to blame for failing to change in response to a transformed social and economic environment. Many of the issues they bargained for in the 1950s and 1960s have become standard operating procedure in large, progressive corporations. As a result, workers today often see joining unions as an unnecessary expense. In the 1970s and

1980s, unions could have reinvented themselves to provide new services to workers but, in general, they chose to continue doing what had worked for them in the past. For example, the voice of the UAW has been absent in calls for reform of the nation's health insurance system. Much like companies that do not change, unions run the risk of self-inflicted extinction. If that were to occur, the American economic and political system might become seriously out of balance, because unions are the most effective check on corporate power, much as the private sector in our democracy is a necessary check on the power of government.

Strong Unions Remain

Although unions are weakened, they are not moribund: they continue to be strong in the hotel and restaurant industries and especially in the public sector, where employers cannot move operations overseas to avoid organization. In some ways, the union bargaining situation with government agencies today is similar to what existed when the UAW7 was the sole union dealing with all American auto companies. At that time, the union could assure carmakers that, if one granted a contract concession, its competitors would have to pay the same labor costs. Unions representing government workers don't have to worry about creating competitive disadvantages among the agencies from which they win concessions. The issue of competition mainly arises when an agency has the option of outsourcing a service to a private employer; typically that isn't feasible with such government services as schools and police.

Overall, it is difficult to know whether employees have a clearer, louder, or stronger voice today than they did in the 1970s. As a result of declining union membership, workers now have a much weaker voice in the political arena. Because they have lost so many dues-paying members, unions simply don't have the funds they once had to lobby the Congress and

167

state legislatures on matters important to all American workers, particularly on matters affecting the poorest-paid and least-educated. In today's workplaces, where bargaining power is based on an employee's skill, knowledge, and access to management rather than on membership in an organized group, employee voice is more individualized. Those employees who can directly address their own personal needs, or the needs of their small workgroups, as opposed to the general needs of fellow union members, benefit. But, for many workers, particularly those in the worst jobs, lacking the collective power of an effective union has meant that not only are they stuck in minimum-wage jobs without benefits, they no longer have the strong voice they once enjoyed in Congress and state legislatures.

Unions Must Improve to Gain Members

Significantly, research shows that most American workers continue to say they like the idea of organized representation, in particular the advantages of collective bargaining, but they are unwilling to join and pay dues to a union. In essence, they are voting with their feet against unions, at least as currently constituted. This leaves open the prospect that, if unions improve their "products" and more effectively address the real concerns of workers in the future, they might be able to regain some of their lost membership and the strength of their voice. But to do so, they will need to rethink their positions and roles relating to such issues as education and training, the individualization of work relationships, and, especially, cooperation with regard to improving business performance.

Immigrants Continue to Work in Dangerous Conditions

Dave Johnson

Dave Johnson has served as an editor and publisher of Industrial Safety & Hygiene News.

One hundred years after the publication of Upton Sinclair's The Jungle, *immigrants, particularly those who are in this country illegally, continue to toil in dangerous conditions. Injuries are all too common, as are on-the-job fatalities. Workers' rights organizations attempt to educate immigrant workers, but in exchange for a paycheck, many immigrants are quite willing to do dangerous jobs and not complain about working conditions. Employers say that America has always depended on immigrants who are willing to do jobs that others will not, but this refrain seems old and tired in the twenty-first century. There is much more work to be done in order to protect all workers in American industries.*

A hundred years ago [in 1906] "The Jungle" was self-published by 27-year-old Upton Sinclair, after rejections from publishers uninterested in a grim novel dedicated to "the workingmen of America." To research his exposé of squalid working conditions in Chicago's meatpacking factories, Sinclair conducted his own hazard recognition walkarounds. Dressed in shabby clothes and carrying a lunch bucket, he wandered the vast Armour facilities unquestioned by what little security existed at the plant.

Jurgis Rudkus, a young, married immigrant from Lithuania, works 12-hour shifts in "The Jungle," sweeping slop and the entrails of butchered cattle into a hole in the floor. The slaughterhouse is dark, filthy and unheated. "The men would tie up their feet in newspapers and old sacks, and these would be covered in blood and frozen," wrote Sinclair. "By nighttime a man would be walking on great lumps the size of the feet of an elephant."

Rudkus sprains his ankle on the floor and spends three months in bed. When the factory refuses to take him back, he finds work at a fertilizer plant, "the foulest place in all Packingtown," where chemicals seep into his skin and Rudkus "smells as foul as the muck."

The Modern Jungle

It's Saturday morning, April 22, 2006. A 20-year-old immigrant from Ecuador, Milton Rocano, climbs into the back of an empty open-top tractor-trailer at a waste recycling transfer station in Brooklyn, N.Y. Without warning, he is buried alive in a cloud of construction debris dumped by a co-worker who doesn't know he's there. The truck dumps the debris and Mr. Rocano's body in a landfill, where it is found three days later after the company and police had tracked it there, as reported in *The New York Times.*

"It was dirty work he did not want to do forever," a friend of Mr. Rocano told the reporter. "It's like he was a dog that was just finished off," said his sister.

On-the-Job Fatalities and Labor Reform

This past August [2006], the Bureau of Labor Statistics reported the number of on-the-job fatalities among Hispanic or Latino workers reached its highest level (917 fatalities) since the census was started in 1992. Workers at the "bottom of the economic ladder are paying a heavy price," said AFL-CIO [American Federation of Labor-Congress of Industrial Organizations] President John Sweeney.

"Today's report is positive news for our nation and all workers," commented OSHA [Occupational Safety and Health

Administration] chief Edwin Foulke, citing an overall decrease in job-related deaths. Alluding to the increase in fatalities among Latinos, African Americans, farm workers and workers under age 20, Foulke added, "there is still more work to do."

OSHA, to its credit, has been doing more in recent years to reach out to Hispanic employers and workers in particular. It has a Spanish-language website, OSHA en Espanol. Compliance assistance tools have been translated into Spanish. The agency provides Spanish-speaking operators on its toll-free "800" telephone number. Training grants are offered to nonprofits to train workers and employers in Spanish to recognize and prevent workplace hazards, and a number of Spanish-language training videos are available.

Of course there is broad reluctance to identify dangerous hazards and negligent employers. "It is not like we are getting any calls or complaints from the community," OSHA regional chief Connors told the *Chicago Tribune* in a September 4th [2006] report.

And trust among members of the Latino community wasn't [bolstered] [in 2005] after Homeland Security officials posed as OSHA representatives, called a "mandatory" safety workshop in North Carolina, and then arrested the workers who showed up.

Statistics underscore the need for much more (and honest) outreach action, beyond what OSHA's limited resources can achieve. A *New York Times* page-one story August 15th [2006] reported immigrants living in U.S. houses rose 16 percent since 2000. The number of immigrants now living in the U.S.—35.7 million; larger than the population of California. Most continue to come from Mexico. But a more recent development has immigrants fanning out throughout the country. Texas, New York, Florida and California have had the largest foreign-born populations, but now states like Georgia, Michigan, Washington, Massachusetts and Montana all show gains in immigrant populations.

Back to the Slaughterhouse

In tiny Postville, Iowa, more than half of the 2,500 residents are Hispanic, according to an article published [in] May [2006] in *The (Weekly) Forward.* The lure? Employment in a large meat plant. The reporter spoke with a Guatemalan woman who works 10–12 hour shifts at the plant, six nights a week, for wages between $6.25 and $7 an hour. Her cutting hand is swollen and deformed, but she has no health insurance to have it checked.

"America has always been built by people . . . willing to do jobs that other people are not willing to do," the plant manager told the reporter. "That's how this country is growing."

That quote could be 100 years old.

Of the 15 industries employing the highest percentage of foreign-born workers, half are low-wage services, including landscaping, domestic household work, car washes, shoe repair and janitorial work, according to a report in the summer 2006 issue of the *City Journal.* The article estimates 100,000 to 300,000 illegal immigrants work as day laborers, many doing home-improvement projects for homeowners or small contractors. (Some years ago I watched a young Mexican plaster sheet rock seams in our newly enclosed carport, working at night by the headlights of his pickup. His wife and baby sat in the front seat, waiting for him.)

Immigrants Still Need Protection

More than 600 people, most of them undocumented Latino immigrants, were hired from street corners to scrub dust off buildings surrounding ground zero after 9/11. They were not told by the private contractors, or by the city, of the dangers involved and were never given PPE [personal protective equipment], reports *The New York Daily News.*

In August [2006], New York Governor George Pataki signed three bills to benefit workers, firefighters, policemen and volunteers who became sick breathing contaminated particles working at ground zero. But many ill immigrants are in danger of being left unprotected. To qualify for benefits they must prove they worked there, and many of the day laborers have no proof. Employers, aware they broke laws by hiring the workers and placing them in dangerous working conditions, are reluctant to help their former employees, according to the *Daily News*.

A hundred years after *The Jungle*, the OSHA chief has it right, regrettably: there is still more work to do. But to Milton Rocano's sister, Manhattan street corner scrubbers, and a Guatemalan in Iowa, that's old news.

Young Women Are Vulnerable to Sexual Harassment in the Workplace

E. J. Graff

E. J. Graff has taught at Brandeis University. She has served as director of the Gender & Justice Project at the Schuster Institute for Investigative Journalism, where she investigates and reports on injustices facing women and children. She has been a senior correspondent for the American Prospect *and a contributor to TPMCafe.com. Her writing has appeared in numerous magazines and newspapers.*

Many teens new to the workplace find themselves unprepared to deal with situations where coworkers or employers act inappropriately. Though there are laws against sexual harassment in the workplace, teens who are used to following orders from superiors may have a difficult time reporting, or even refusing, inappropriate advances. Parents must be proactive with their teenage wage earners and take steps to ensure that their children are safe from workplace predators. Ultimately, the best way to end sexual harassment in the workplace is to use the legal system to make sure that companies follow the law regarding workplace sexual harassment.

At first, 16-year-old Maureen Smith [name changed to protect privacy] loved her new job at UltraStar Cinemas' Poway 10 theater. It was fun to see movies for free, and she liked goofing around with the other kids who worked there, including her best friend, Lindsay. Maureen's parents had been pleased when she'd told them she wanted an after-school job so she could earn her own spending money. At the time, Mau-

E. J. Graff, "Is Your Daughter Safe at Work?" *Good Housekeeping*, vol. 244, no. 6, June 2007, pp. 162–164, 224, 226. Copyright © 2007 Hearst Communications. Reproduced by permission of Schuster Institute for Investigative Journalism.

reen was a high school junior who not only earned academic awards, but played lacrosse and ran cross-country. Yet her mother, Katherine, felt her daughter could handle the new responsibility: "She was very disciplined," Katherine recalls.

A few weeks after Maureen started working at the San Diego–area theater, Dan Wooten, 32, was brought in to become general manager—and everything changed. "Dan had an air about him that was really intimidating," Maureen says now. His language was foul—"I heard words out of him that I'd never heard from anyone in my entire life"—and his favorite topic was sex. He would describe his own sex life in disturbingly graphic detail. He would point out customers and ask the girls who worked at the theater whether they'd want to have sex with those men. And he showed off the pornographic magazines that he had stashed in the box office.

Continued Harassment

Dan wasn't the only problem. The assistant manager, Adam Gustafson, physically harassed Maureen and the other girls. He'd grab them abruptly, bending their arms into painful positions, then put them in armlocks—restraint holds he was learning at the police academy and practicing, he said. Or he'd come up from behind, tilt their stools back suddenly so they'd be terrified they'd hit the floor, then catch them against his hips.

But for Maureen, the worst part was that Dan kept scheduling her to work at night—in the box office, often alone with him. There, he'd make sexually provocative remarks, telling her that he liked the way her hips moved when she walked, for example. He'd also touch her, rubbing her flat stomach admiringly or taking her wrist and commenting on how "little" it was. When she cut her hair, he got extremely upset, and said that women were sexier with long hair and that cutting it was a "sin."

Although Maureen found it embarrassing and degrading to have Dan treat her this way, she tried to ignore it, hoping that would make him stop. She also felt confused. From time to time, other managers came through the theater, and she and Lindsay would try to tell them what was happening. But the managers merely shrugged. Maureen became afraid of not being taken seriously. "I just thought that was how the real world was," she says.

The Dangerous Boss

Many parents worry about the threat of sexual predators on the Internet and try to monitor their kids' online activity. That threat is real, and yet teens are far more likely to encounter a predator on the job. While no one can say exactly how widespread the problem is, a 2005 study from the University of Southern Maine reported that 46 percent of teenage girls who'd worked had been sexually harassed: three percent had been victims of sexual assault or attempted assault or rape. And lawyers for the federal Equal Employment Opportunity Commission (EEOC) say they've been seeing more and more of these harassment cases over the past several years— all over the country. Because of the spike, the commission recently launched its first educational initiative aimed at teens and their employers.

Although the Maine study was small, the numbers are not surprising: Other research has shown that the younger the worker and the lower she is in the hierarchy, the more likely she is to be harassed. And the numbers are in line with a 1994 survey, still considered definitive, of adult women working in federal agencies. That study found that 44 percent of women in the agencies had faced some form of unwanted sexual attention on the job.

Most often, teens work at low-wage restaurant, retail, or service jobs, where they're likely to be supervised by transient managers who are themselves low-skilled, inadequately trained, and poorly paid. Their bosses too often ignore sexually tinged behavior, dismissing it as harmless flirtation and not recognizing that predators are unlikely to back off. Indeed, psychologists say that the men are often seeing how much they can get away with, pushing further each time.

Ignoring the Law

Managers are also ignoring the law. In most states, if sexual harassment includes unwanted touching, it could be a criminal offense. And under federal law, it's a civil offense for which the employer can be sued. Most states and some municipalities have additional laws on the books that safeguard employees.

If bosses won't protect underage workers, then parents must. That means alerting your child to the risks when she starts hunting for her first job and staying watchful once she begins.

This goes for sons as well as daughters. Although girls are more vulnerable, boys can be victims, too, as evidenced when Representative Mark Foley of Florida was caught sending suggestive e-mails and sexually explicit instant messages to male congressional pages.

Afraid to Talk Back

In the Foley case, it was a young page who blew the whistle. But it's rare for teens to come forward. A part-time job is usually their first foray into the adult world, and they're eager to appear grown-up, responsible, able to handle whatever happens.

What's more, predators often target the polite, obedient, well-behaved "good girls," explains Christine Nicholson, Ph.D., a clinical psychologist in Albuquerque, NM, who specializes in adolescent girls and sexual trauma. "These are the ones who say, 'Please, can I do anything for you?'" Men know they can manipulate these girls—and that, like Maureen, they're likely to respond with silence.

Not that the system makes it easy for young victims to speak up. Federal sexual harassment law allows all employees to file a complaint, but it doesn't make any special allowances for teenagers. A lawsuit is likely to be stronger if a victim has complained—if not to the harasser, then to her supervisor or to Human Resources or another designated person. But most teenagers won't do that. "They're used to doing what Mom and Dad say, what their teachers say, what their coaches say," explains Jennifer Drobac, an Indiana University law professor and former employment attorney. "Yet the legal system expects these girls to confront their first workplace authority figure and say, 'That's completely inappropriate conduct on your part.'"

Deborah Healy, who worked as a cashier at a Burlington Coat Factory in Springfield, IL, found it very hard to stand up for herself. A manager had repeatedly asked her personal questions that made her uncomfortable. And one time, when she was alone with him in a locked room as he counted out her cash drawer, he insisted that she sit on his lap. "I just did it," says Deb, who was 17 at the time. "I sat on his leg—really lightly—for a second and then ran to the other side of the room. I thought that was my only option."

Reluctance to Report Harassment

Yet a month later, when a higher-up manager told her that the man was being fired for sexual harassment and asked Deb whether she had anything to tell them, she was reluctant to talk about the incident. "I didn't want to be the one to ruin the man's life," she explains. That may sound strange, but Deb was young, naive, and so ashamed of the encounter that, like many unprepared girls, "I sort of felt responsible for what had happened," she says.

A girl may also worry about losing her job. Natoshia Hanneken worked at a Burger King in Peerless Park, MO, as part of a school-based work-study program. A senior in high school, she not only got paid for her hours, she earned credits toward graduation. Every day after morning classes, Natoshia and her friend Bethany [name changed to protect privacy] headed to work.

Almost immediately, their shift manager, Nathan Kraus, started to annoy them. Some of it was verbal—for example, asking the girls to head out to the Dumpster with him for sex. Or if one of them was kneeling down to wipe the floor, he'd say things like. "As long as you're down there, you can do me a favor."

But Nathan also got physical, swiping their breasts and bottoms with his hand as he walked by, pinning Bethany against a wall and groping her breasts, bumping and grinding against Natoshia's bottom as she bent over to get barbecue sauce for a customer. Still, she and Bethany felt they had to try to get along with him. "Our graduation depended on this job," says Natoshia. "We couldn't quit. We couldn't get fired."

Getting Someone to Listen

And yet, Natoshia wasn't afraid to confront her boss. Over and over, she told him to cut it out. "You need to stop saying this stuff to me because I find it really disgusting," she said. Within a week, she and Bethany reported him to a higher-up manager. The girls didn't know it at the time, but other young workers had also complained about Nathan's behavior. Yet, incredibly, the manager "didn't seem to believe us," says Natoshia. After that, she and Bethany found an internal complaint hotline. The man who answered the phone, says Natoshia, "told us that maybe we were taunting [Nathan] with our body language and by the way we were wearing our uniforms."

The girls felt desperate. Although one shift manager was sympathetic, no one did anything about the situation. Wherever they turned, they were being blamed—not the creep who was tormenting them.

Natoshia began to fall apart. Once she'd been proud of her long blond hair. But as soon as Nathan admired it, she cut it as short as she could and dyed it a gloomy brown. She got a nose ring, a belly ring, a tongue ring. Looking back, Natoshia sees that she was silently "screaming out for help, too afraid to ask out loud."

The Aftermath of Harassment

Finally, Bethany told her older sister, who got the girls an appointment with a lawyer. The appointment was scheduled for the morning, and Natoshia, ever the dutiful girl, did not want to miss school without a parent's note. So she finally told her mom what had been going on. "It felt really, really good that someone listened to us and believed us," says Natoshia.

The lawyer took the case, and the EEOC, after investigating and concluding that the law had been violated, filed a lawsuit, with seven girls as plaintiffs. In December 2004, Midamerica Hotels Corporation and Northwest Development Company, which operated that Burger King (along with 37 others), settled for $400,000 in damages.

But the girls didn't feel vindicated. Although the company had to agree to EEOC oversight for two years, there was no admission of wrongdoing. Nathan Kraus had been allowed to resign earlier, and one of the assistant managers, while initially reprimanded, was later promoted to manager. (Then, as part of the settlement, he was required to go for sexual harassment-awareness training.)

The legal process itself was brutal. During the mediation talks, Nathan would stare the girls down: when the groups went into separate rooms (as part of the talks), he would pace the hall just outside the girls' room, smirking at them.

Today, Natoshia is still struggling and has dropped her plans to go to nursing school. Since high school, she has held a series of jobs, and by her own admission, she currently has no boyfriend and only a few girlfriends. "Once something like this happens, it changes your whole perspective on everything," she says.

Ending Harassment Through the Legal Process

Maureen Smith's problems at the movie theater got worse before they got better. After Maureen began dating Travis, an 18-year-old student whom she'd met through her church group and who had also worked at the theater, Dan Wooten became even more lewd. Then one night, Maureen came home late and thought that she spotted Dan's car on her street. As the garage door closed, her cell phone rang. It was Dan. He asked where she'd been, what she'd been doing, and why she was getting home so late. He'd become a stalker.

But it took a serious injury before Maureen and Lindsay finally broke down and told their parents what they'd been going through. Lindsay needed emergency medical treatment because Adam, the assistant manager, dislocated her shoulder when he pulled her into one of his arm holds—in horseplay, he later claimed. The parents reported the men to the local police, but when no charges were filed, Maureen, Lindsay, and two other girls brought a civil lawsuit against UltraStar Cinemas' management.

Following an eight-week trial, in April 2005, a jury found unanimously in the girls' favor and awarded $850,000 for emotional distress and another $1.5 million each in punitive damages—a total of $6.85 million. That July, the judge threw out the damage award as excessive and ordered a new trial on the monetary issue only. The case is currently on appeal in the California courts. But the finding of harassment is not under question.

Today, Maureen is about to graduate from college. Thinking about what she and Lindsay went through can still bring her to tears. But the girls decided to tell their story, they say, to prevent the same thing from happening to other girls.

As a result of her ordeal, Maureen has decided to become a lawyer specializing in sexual harassment cases. "The best way to stop it," she says, "is to make companies realize that they need to take action against it. And the best way to do that is through the legal process."

She knows that the work won't be easy, but she remembers clearly what kept her going during the stressful litigation and its aftermath. "Every time I wanted to stop," she says, "I thought about the fact that Dan might go back—and that there might be other Dans out there doing the same thing right now."

Globalization Exploits Child Labor

Sarah Cox

Sarah Cox is a journalist based in Victoria, British Columbia, who writes about globalization.

Around the world millions of children, some as young as five years old, toil to make goods for the United States and other major markets. They often work excessive hours, seven days per week. In most countries the minimum wage for children is far less than that for adults, and these young workers often bring home a pittance for their arduous labor. Many of these children also work at jobs that are deemed hazardous—meaning that the work causes irreparable physical or psychological damage. The products children make are sold by major U.S. corporations, and though there have been crackdowns, companies are slow to demand reforms unless the abuses are uncovered by outside agencies.

Tariq was 12 years old when he had a fleeting month of fame. In 1996, a *Life* magazine photographer found him in a Pakistani village sewing panels on Nike soccer balls for 79 cents a ball. Tariq helped push the issue of child labour into the international spotlight. In the fallout, Nike and other companies were forced to adopt codes of conduct that would prevent kids from making their products.

Yet child labour, fostered by the new global economy, remains pervasive. Companies bent on earning ever-higher profits demand ever-lower production costs. They squeeze producers to make more for less. In turn, producers often look for the cheapest employees—children. The International Labour Organization estimates 180 million children aged five to 17 are engaged in the worst forms of hazardous labour: work that causes irreversible physical or psychological damage, or even threatens their lives. That's one in eight children worldwide. An additional 67 million aged five to 14 do work that hinders their education, development and future livelihoods. When researchers ask child labourers how they want to spend their days, the answer is almost always the same: "I want to go to school."

Rotten Bananas

The friendly stickers on the ever-popular banana carry familiar brand names like Del Monte, Chiquita and Dole. Many also say "Ecuador," the world's biggest exporter of North America's favourite fruit. What the stickers don't tell you is that child labour is widespread on Ecuadorian banana fields and packing plants. Human Rights Watch reports that children as young as eight years old work 12 hours a day for an average $4.72 per day—that's 60% of the legal minimum wage for adult banana workers. Children's jobs include wrapping insecticide-treated plastic around banana stalks and cutting yellow leaves from plants with machetes, according to the group's 2002 report, "Tainted Harvest". The young workers also learn to do their work with one hand while shielding themselves from fungicides sprayed from planes with the other.

Pre-shrunk Labour

Most of the estimated 450,000 children who labour in the pesticide-coated cottonseed fields of south India are girls aged six to 14. About 95% are bonded labourers who toil up to 13 hours a day to pay off loans their parents owe the employers. The seeds are produced and marketed by local subsidiaries of multinationals like Monsanto and Unilever, according to a 2003 study commissioned by the India Committee of the Netherlands, Child Labour and Trans-National Seed Compa-

Union workers and other protestors rally outside a New York City outlet of The Gap on January 31, 2001. They are accusing Gap and other businesses of exploiting workers in other countries, and demanding reforms in the global economy. AP Images.

nies in Hybrid Cottonseed Production in Andhra Pradesh. If you see a tag with "100% cotton" on it, ask if that's hybrid or genetically modified. If so, chances are a child in debt bondage pollinated the plant that made the seed, that grew the crop, that produced the cotton, that made the shirt.

Unhappy Meals

"No-one cares more about kids and their safety than McDonald's," claims the golden arches' website. But when children were discovered making Happy-Meal toys in China [in 2001], it looked like McDonald's reputation as a champion of children's health and welfare was, well, fried. Youngsters aged 12 and 13 had been recruited from the Gun-Zhi-Yi-Zhong high school in Guangdong province to put clothes on plastic Aladdin toys. They toiled at City Toys, owned by Hong Kong–based McDonald's supplier Pleasure Tech Holdings. During peak seasons, workers laboured up to 14 hours a day for as little as 30 cents an hour. The children were sent back to their school after three days, but 14 and 15 year olds continued to make plastic Winnie the Poohs and Hello-Kitties in violation of Chinese labour law, according to the Hong Kong Christian Industrial Committee. Following an exposé in the *South China Sunday Morning Post*, an inspection team was sent to the factory. When McDonald's cancelled its contract with City Toys, hundreds of underage workers were fired. Later, McDonald's denied children ever made its promotional toys.

Not Having a Ball

An estimated 25,000 children aged 10 to 14 stitch soccer balls in India's Punjab region and in Pakistan around the colonial city of Sialkot, reports the Global March Against Child Labour. The two countries are leading exporters of sporting goods. Hexagonal panels are cut in factories and, to save on labour costs, "kits" of 32 panels per ball are shipped to slums and villages for assembly. Children are prized for their nimble fingers and obedience. They are also paid considerably less than adult sewers, who themselves make a daily average of just $1.44.

Nike, Adidas and other bigwig manufacturers have pledged to monitor production and help rehabilitate child labourers and bring them to school. But Global March says neither the companies nor the International Federation of Football Associations have done nearly enough. The coalition wants manufacturers to agree to a transparent, industry-wide monitoring system and a tracking system for production.

Rags for Richies

If the tag on your kid's jeans says "made in Mexico," they could be from Tehuacan, a valley city in Puebla state that used to be surrounded by cornfields. These days, Tehuacan is surrounded by more than 400 low-wage maquiladoras [factories] that produce denim clothing for companies like Levi Strauss, Wal-Mart, The Limited and Tommy Hilfiger.

If you stroll through Tehuacan's streets at shift-change, you're sure to find 13 and 14 year olds who sew jeans. When inspectors come, the children hide, reports the Human and Labour Rights Commission of the Tehuacan Valley. Children are also illegally employed in home-based sewing facilities subcontracted by factories, says the Maquila Solidarity Network. Adult maquila workers make about $50 a week; they would need three times that to meet the basic needs of a typical family. Many live in shacks without running water or electricity. So far none of the multinationals sourcing in Tehuacan have used their clout to improve wages for adults so their children can go to school.

Tricky Treats

Life is like a box of chocolates and chances are the key ingredient, cocoa, was grown and harvested with child labour. More than a quarter of a million children as young as six work in West Africa's cocoa industry, reports the Nigeria-based International Institute of Tropical Agriculture. On Ivory Coast plantations, which supply 40% of the world's cocoa, an estimated 15,000 children are slaves kidnapped by traders or lured with false promises of high pay. For up to 18 hours a day, children use machetes to harvest cocoa beans from jungle farms. Without masks or other protective equipment, they spray crops with insecticides and pesticides. Farmers claim they rely on underage labourers because they are paid so little for their crops that they cannot afford adult wages. Global chocolatiers like Nestle and Hershey's have pledged to take steps to end child labour in the industry by 2005. In the meantime, you can sample slave-free chocolate from health food stores or your local fair trade organization.

The Mouse Rules

In Bangladesh, kids work 14 hours a day sewing Disney children's clothes. New York–based National Labor Committee reports that despite a 1995 agreement that imposed fines on companies employing children, teenagers still stitch for Disney. Lisa Rahman began sewing seams on Disney clothes at Bangladesh's Shah Makhdum factory when she was 16. Rahman worked 8 a.m. to 10 p.m. seven days a week for 19 cents an hour. When worker abuses were exposed at the factory [in 2003], Disney yanked production. A chagrined Shah Makdhum owner apologized to his 352 workers, made drastic improvements and agreed to independent monitoring. But the Mouse has refused to reinstate production orders. The National Labor Committee believes this is because Disney fears independent monitoring could set a costly precedent for tens of thousands of factories that churn out its cartoon wares.

Global Workers Must Have a Voice

Lisa Roner

Lisa Roner has served as North American editor of Ethical Corporation.

All over the world, workers in global supply chains provide parts, items, and goods that end up being sold in the United States. But they are not accorded the wages or rights of U.S. workers. Allowing these laborers to unionize would be a step toward seeing that minimum labor standards are met. Many U.S. corporations make huge profits from goods made in foreign supply chains, and, while they may advocate for better working conditions abroad, their actions do not always coincide with their press releases. Corporations' historically strained relationship with domestic labor unions may be hindering the creation of workers' advocacy groups abroad. All workers should have a voice, and U.S. corporations need to take steps to enable foreign workers in supply chains to be heard.

For more than a decade [since the mid-90s], technology, clothing and other sectors with globe-spanning supply chains have been implementing codes of conduct and monitoring compliance through auditing. Today, there is growing consensus among activists, academic researchers and many brands and retailers that the results fall short of the ambition of broadly improving conditions.

Not Enough Is Being Done for Labor Rights

Without the ability to maintain "sustainable supervision" in factories through unions or other forms of independent workers' organisations, labour rights experts predict sustainable improvements will remain elusive. Despite brands' strong commitments in principle to workers' freedom of association, few successful trade unions exist in supplier factories in the developing nations that are the core of the manufacturing industries.

Are companies as committed to workers' rights to organise as they profess?

Labour rights experts say the economic squeeze companies place on factories proves they are disingenuous when it comes to their support for the formation of unions. But many large US companies believe other forms of worker representation, especially in countries such as China where independent labour organisations are forbidden by law, better serve workers' immediate needs.

The current system of audits and continuous assessment to ensure suppliers uphold minimum labour standards is not working, says Dara O'Rourke, associate professor of environmental and labour policy at the University of California, Berkeley.

Recurring instances of the same problems in yearly audits at the same factories and increasing awareness of the ability of factories to "game" the system by coaching workers and maintaining multiple sets of books have left a whole range of "actors looking for a 'version 3.0' of auditing", O'Rourke says.

More than Monitoring

Jill Esbenshade, assistant professor of sociology at San Diego State University, agrees that auditing and monitoring have not resulted in "widespread amelioration of the kinds of conditions that brought monitoring on in the first place".

The problems, however, run deeper than the complexities and logistical difficulties of monitoring systems, says Scott Nova, executive director of the Worker Rights Consortium, a non-profit organisation comprising more than 100 colleges and universities committed to fighting sweatshop labour abuses.

There is a reason, he says, that most labour rights advocates view association rights as the single most important element of a code of conduct. When that right is respected, experts agree, it creates a robust and powerful mechanism within the factory to promote compliance with every other code provision.

But it costs more to produce under good conditions than bad, he says, and during the ten years since codes came on the scene, production costs have increased while prices at the factory door have fallen.

Buyers must recognise factories that take action to improve worker's rights, says Kevin Kolben, assistant professor of accounting and information systems at Rutgers Business School, and be willing to "pay the extra pennies" to support that effort.

Nova believes brands also must consolidate their supply chains to ensure they are the primary customer of the factories whose fundamental management practices they are trying to alter.

Hollow Promises?

Brands' unwillingness to take these fairly simple steps, Kolben says, "reflects a lack of commitment to the goal" and reinforces many labour rights advocates' beliefs that the primary purpose of codes in the eyes of retailers is not to protect workers but to preserve brand reputation.

O'Rourke, however, says that while some companies are doing audits just for the sake of the public relations points it earns them, others are truly struggling to clean up their supply chains, spending lots of money and still not reaching their goals. Success, he says, requires totally different mechanisms focused on empowering workers.

He advocates an approach to monitoring that applies attributes of lean manufacturing—such as competitiveness, productivity, quality, timeliness and flexibility—to compliance. "Lean compliance," O'Rourke says, relies on better measurement and root cause analysis, coupled with a commitment to continuous improvement that has been lacking in "check-list" audits.

The approach, O'Rourke says, includes benchmarking and creating learning systems across the supply chain.

Independent labour unions or other forms of worker organisation are still vital though, say O'Rourke and Nova.

Esbenshade, however, sees a "real reluctance" by manufacturers to work with unionised factories. Nova agrees and says that despite formal commitments to associational rights around the world, the stance being taken by most US companies is vigorously anti-union.

"It would not be surprising if hostility to unions in the domestic context spilled over into a lack of enthusiasm for defending associational rights in the global supply chain," Nova says.

Kolben says US companies are resistant to unions in the developing world because of preconceptions and bad experiences with US unions. In addition, he says companies are ill-equipped to compel contractors that have their own anti-union sentiments to work more with organised labour.

Ken Larson, principal of Ken Larson Consulting and former director of corporate responsibility at Hewlett-Packard, says that although there is a small but growing recognition among some companies that unions may be part of the answer, at most, talk of unions is considered "treasonous".

"That bias is very much alive, particularly among corporate executives, but it's not a very well thought out rationale," he says.

Doug Cahn, principal of corporate responsibility consultancy TheCahnGroup and former vice-president for human

A boy works at a welding machine at a factory in Allahabad, India, in 2004. Many goods sold in America are made overseas, where child labor and other forms of worker exploitation are common. AP Images.

rights programmes at Reebok, agrees that commitments of US companies towards freedom of association are tarnished by the contentious history of labour management relations.

Giving Workers a Voice

Workers need a voice, the influence and the ability to negotiate over the problems they think are the most important, O'Rourke says. And although the most obvious form of that voice is a union, particularly in countries where the political environment precludes unions, workers still must be included "in a serious way", he says.

The current system of supply chain monitoring, O'Rourke says, creates incentives for factories to hide problems and to give an illusion that all is well. Instead, incentives for airing problems and solving them through collaboration are needed that put workers at the centre of problem identification and resolution.

"Brands and retailers must do some serious work to create the space to facilitate workers' participation in risky ventures, including issues related to wages, overtime, and health and safety, particularly in countries like China and Vietnam," O'Rourke warns.

He says companies must not simply offer a union that looks like a US union, but must examine best practice today for worker participation.

Despite an aversion to formal trade unions, Larson says that in the technology sector there is a strong commitment to employee representation that gives workers a voice. Most companies, he says, believe the best solutions are based on good employee management communications, and many say that can be accomplished without a union.

Current best practice is to establish protocols to open up employee-manager communication, particularly through employee health and safety committees, he says.

"I think that's the mode that people are moving toward and even that is a big step for a lot of plant managers," Larson says. "Brands and the mainline manufacturers running the supply chains are all pretty committed to that."

One corporate responsibility manager for a UK fashion brand operating in Asia says most brand managers believe worker-led health and safety committees are a valuable alternative to the "freaking out" of management over union issues. Management training and worker education programmes can be just as helpful in getting results, without union contention, she says.

Larson says brands and factory owners realise that such approaches help to blunt some of the union effort. If workers feel they have a voice and see things being remedied, the need for a union diminishes somewhat, he says.

Cahn says there is "no shortage of activity to raise awareness and to create some fundamental initiatives to respect the right of freedom of association", although tremendous challenges remain in every country. And while he acknowledges such efforts fall short of the promotion of trade unions, he believes they go well beyond "ignoring the freedom of association requirement".

It would be helpful to learn from unions what they view as the beneficial interim steps to unionisation, Larson says. Right now, he says, there is an "all or nothing" approach.

Such steps are just part of the solution, however, Cahn says. The sustained protection of workers also relies on governments doing their part to nurture trade union access and a commitment from unions to develop in ways that are reflective of worker's needs, he believes.

Kolben agrees and says that the US and other governments should be working not only to encourage and create incentives to ensure that core labour rights are enforced in supplier countries, but also to focus on how labour rights are incorporated into the main provisions of trade agreements.

Making a Stand

Kolben says a better case needs to be made for why unions can be good for business. Brands and retailers should consider the benefit that worker organisations could bring in countries such as China, suggests O'Rourke.

Independent global unions say they can spur true "bottom-up" worker representation and negotiate collective agreements that cover all major conditions in the workplace, while still working within the confines of the official Chinese trade union structure.

Global union UNI says that when workers' rights and interests are properly protected, a company's workers and the union are empowered to help the development of transnational organisations in environments such as China.

The fear in such a country, O'Rourke says, is not that the workers will be extorting you, but more that local officials and factory managers will be. Having a legitimate worker body, he urges, is not that costly and is potentially quite positive for firms.

Cahn agrees that buyers can and should impose an environment on factories where workers are not intimidated to raise their voices and where unions can have access to workers who desire to seek association.

Nova holds out, however, that the biggest obstacle to workers' ability to organise is the economic squeeze that brands and retailers place on factories. Even when companies step in to support the formation of independent unions or worker organisations, if labour rights concessions result in factories being unable to remain competitive on price, quality and delivery time, he says, the result may be a loss of jobs.

Until brands encourage factories to support freedom of association and stand behind those that do for the long term, even if it means modest price increases, labour rights scholars say no substantial progress can be expected on association and the broader array of code standards.

"We've only scratched the surface of eliminating the fear, creating credible unions around the world and promoting the responsible behaviour of buyers and factory managers," Cahn says.

And the anti-union "home culture" defines US companies' perspectives, he says, giving US brands a potentially steeper experiential curve to go through than their European counterparts. The good news, however, Cahn says, is that the journey along that curve is well underway.

Women's Salaries Continue to Lag Behind Men's

Aaron Bernstein

Aaron Bernstein has served as a senior writer for Business Week *where he covered workplace and social issues. He is the author of the book* Grounded: Frank Lorenzo and the Destruction of Eastern Airlines *and coauthor of* In the Company of Owners: The Truth About Stock Options.

Despite seeming improvements in women's pay versus that of their male counterparts, women still trail men when it comes to compensation for similar labor. Statistics that show marked improvements can be deceiving, because they are often based on women who hold full-time jobs continuously, while a large percentage of women do not do so in our society, opting instead to take time off for child care. Women tend to get equivalent treatment to men in the workplace when they act most like men and do not let domestic duties sidetrack them. Thus, we still live in a sex-segregated society when it comes to compensation for labor. The pay gap does continue to shrink, but significant gains will be slow in coming until workplaces become more family friendly.

During the heyday of the women's movement more than 30 years ago [in the early 70s], "59 cents on the dollar" was an oft-heard rallying cry, referring to how little women earned compared with men. Those concerns seem outdated today, when it's easy to find female doctors, lawyers, pop stars, even Presidential advisers. The progress toward equality in the workplace also shows up in government data on wages, which pegs women's average pay at 77% of men's compensation today.

Deceiving Statistics

But there's new evidence that women's advances may not be quite so robust after all. When you look at how much the typical woman actually earns over much of her career, the true figure is more like 44% of what the average man makes. That's the conclusion of a . . . study by Stephen J. Rose, an economist at Macro International Inc., a consulting firm, and Heidi I. Hartmann, President of the Institute for Women's Policy Research in Washington.

Why the big discrepancy? The Bureau of Labor Statistics (BLS) numbers, published every year, are accurate as far as they go. But they only measure the earnings of those who work full-time for an entire year. Only one-quarter of women, though, achieve this level of participation consistently throughout their working lives. So Rose and Hartmann looked at the pay of all men and women over 15 years, including those who worked part-time and dipped in and out of the labor force to care for children or elderly parents. This long-term perspective still shows an arc of progress: The 44%, based on average earnings between 1983 and 1998, jumped from 29% in the prior 15 years. But the more comprehensive view gives a less rosy picture of women's position in the work world.

Reasons for Unequal Pay

Outright discrimination against women probably accounts for only about 10 percentage points of the pay gap, according to numerous studies. The bulk of the problem, then, lies with the conflicting needs and norms of society and employers. A majority of men and women still work in largely sex-segregated occupations, Rose and Hartmann's study shows, leaving many women stuck in lower-paying jobs such as cashiers and maids.

Family responsibilities, too, typically still fall more heavily on women, and neither society nor employers have found good ways to mesh those with job demands. Rose and

Hartmann's data show that women can get equal treatment today—but mostly when they behave like traditional men and leave the primary family responsibilities at home. For the majority who can't or won't do that, the work world remains much less accommodating. Of course, many women choose to take time off or to work part-time to be with their children rather than stay on the job. Yet that choice itself is constrained by the widespread lack of day care and flexible job options, Hartmann argues. "The 44% gap we found shows that there are still tremendous differences in how the labor market treats men and women," she says.

Hartmann and Rose came to their results by examining long-term earnings trends. The 77% figure comes from the BLS's 2002 earnings survey and looks at how much full-time, year-round workers make in a given year. By contrast, Rose and Hartmann used a University of Michigan survey that has tracked a sample of randomly chosen people and their children since 1968. They looked at how much each person made between 1983 and 1998 in every year from age 26 to 59 (to exclude students and retirees).

The Penalty for Child Care

One surprise was just how many women work most of their adult lives. Fully 96% of these prime-age women worked at least one of those 15 years, and they clocked an average of 12 years on the job. In other words, few women these days drop out altogether once they have kids.

But those few years out of the labor market carry a stiff penalty. More than half of all women spent at least a year out of the labor force, the study found, and they earned an average of $21,363 a year over the years they worked, after inflation adjustments, vs. nearly $30,000 for women who stuck with it for all 15 years. Indeed, anyone who drops out risks derailing their career and permanently slashing their pay. Just one year off cuts a woman's total earnings over 15 years by

32%, while two years slice it by 46% and three by 56%, according to Hartmann and Rose. The work world penalizes men nearly as much; their average pay drops by 25% if they take off a year. Fewer than 8% of men did so, however. "Our economic system is still based on a family division of labor, and women pay the price," says Rose.

Women also take a big hit for going part-time. On average, they work a lot less than men: 1,498 hours a year, vs. 2,219 worked by the typical man. The fewer hours women work account for about half of the total pay gap between the sexes, Rose and Hartmann concluded. Some women have turned to self-employment as a way to fit work and family together. But they often must accept lower pay in the process. Brita Bergland, a Windsor (Vt.) resident, found it difficult to manage her sales job at a printing company while she also cared for her aging mother and her daughter. So she struck out on her own and has managed the work-life balance much better ever since. The cost: about a $15,000 cut in annual earnings, down from the $55,000 to $60,000 she made as an employee. "These are the choices women make because society doesn't help them to support children and parents," says Bergland, who's now 50.

A Sex-Segregated Economy

And while many women have made great strides in some highly visible professions such as law and medicine, historical patterns of sex segregation remain strong across much of the economy. Overall, just 15% of women work in jobs typically held by men, such as engineer, stockbroker, and judge, while fewer than 8% of men hold female-dominated jobs such as nurse, teacher, or sales clerk. These findings were reiterated in a detailed BLS analysis that uses the 2000 census to look at the jobs men and women hold.

Such a sex-segregated economy leaves women with some startling disadvantages. Overall, they earn less than men with the same education at all levels. Incredibly, male dropouts pulled down an average of $36,000 a year between 1983 and 1998, after inflation adjustments, while women with a bachelor's degree made $35,000. Women with a graduate degree averaged $42,000, but men got nearly $77,000.

The Good News

The good news is that the pay gap continues to narrow no matter how it's measured. That's likely to continue; female college graduation rates surpass those of men, and they're catching up in grad school, too, so they're likely to gain from an economy that rewards skill. Women also should benefit from the ongoing shift to services, where they're more likely to work, and lose less than men from the decline of factory jobs.

Still, speedier progress probably won't happen without more employers making work sites family-friendly and revamping jobs to accommodate women and men as they seek to balance work and family demands. "The workplace needs to change to match the workforce," says Ellen Bravo, national director of 9to5, National Association of Working Women. Until that happens, a woman's labor will continue to be worth a fraction of a man's.

Whistleblowers May Be as Fraudulent as the Corporations They Accuse

Alexei Oreskovic

Alexei Oreskovic has been a reporter at the Recorder, *a San Francisco affiliate of* Texas Lawyer.

With some highly publicized cases in the early 2000s, whistleblowers, or those who provide information about corporate abuses, have ascended to a revered status. However, this occurrence, along with new laws that protect those who speak out, has opened the door for workers to abuse the system themselves. In particular, marginal or poorly performing employees may work the system to cover up their own inadequacies and protect their jobs, because whistleblowers are protected by the law. Corporations must now institute policies that protect workers' rights at the same time as they protect against frivolous complaints.

Two-and-a-half years after the Enron Corp. accounting scandal [in 2002], whistleblowers are practically national heroes.

Time magazine crowned a trio of whistleblowers its persons of the year in 2002—one was former Enron executive Sherron Watkins—and the Sarbanes-Oxley Corporate Fraud and Accountability Act of 2002, passed the same year, codified various protections for workers who blow the whistle.

New Challenges

But the rise of the whistleblower also has created a new set of challenges for some employment lawyers. While whistleblower protections have proven effective for uncovering corporate fraud, they're also an alluring cloak for poorly performing workers to drape over themselves when the going gets tough.

The delicate nature of these situations, and the high stakes involved—including stiff criminal and civil penalties—is forcing employment attorneys to revise some of their tactics and to widen the circle of lawyers involved.

"These things are so problematic because they involve not only the human resources [HR] issue of nonretaliation, but they now raise this much broader panorama of issues," says Victor Schachter, an employment partner in San Francisco's Fenwick & West.

In one incident, recalls Schachter, an employee whose job performance had increasingly come under criticism made allegations of accounting improprieties within the company.

The allegations set the wheels in motion for an accounting investigation, while at the same time threatening to halt an imminent evaluation of the employee's own performance— any adverse action could have been interpreted as evidence of retaliation for blowing the whistle.

Suddenly, intertwined in what traditionally has been an employment law situation were a knot of other concerns. In the incident, the whistleblowing claim turned out to be legitimate, but the company still negotiated the employee's termination.

An Explosion of Claims

The situation has become increasingly common, says Schachter.

"I've seen a mini-explosion of whistleblower claims by people who are marginal performers, if not malingerers," he says.

"It's not an everyday occurrence, but it's an occurrence that goes on in the workplace on a regular basis," says Linda Headley, managing shareholder in the Houston office of employment firm Littler Mendelson.

Under Sarbanes-Oxley, an employee who provides information or assists in an investigation relating to a company's violation of federal fraud laws or Securities and Exchange Commission rules cannot be fired or discriminated against for coming forward. And the allegation need not turn out to be legitimate so long as the employee "reasonably believes" it to be a violation.

True Claims or Sour Grapes?

Charles Wilson, a senior associate with Epstein Becker Green Wickliff and Hall in Houston, says whistleblowing to protect a job may be more common today, but it's not a new development.

"I've been involved in plenty of situations where you have an employee who knows they are either a marginal or poor performer—they see the writing on the wall—and then they make up this claim of 'I've been discriminated against,' for instance," Wilson says.

"The key to dealing with that is you have to take each and every claim seriously, regardless of whether this person is making it up," he says.

Worker advocates say attempts to portray whistleblowers as inept employees underscore the need for whistleblower protections.

Jeffrey Ross, a plaintiffs attorney at Oakland's Dickson Ross, says his experience has been that "once high-performing, well-respected employees blow the whistle, suddenly they become, in retrospect, terrible, if not incompetent, employees."

"It's a very typical response," adds Ross, who says he's seen a sharp rise in the number of whistleblower retaliation cases his firm handles.

John E. Clark, of counsel at Goode Casseb Jones Riklin Choate & Watson in San Antonio [Texas] who represents whistleblowers in qui tam litigation [private lawsuits against corporate fraud] says he never has represented anyone who is a poor performer on the job and is using a whistle-blowing claim to protect his or her job.

"Typically the whistleblower goes to the employer and says, 'Hey, can we do this?' and are told to mind their business," he says.

Ripe for Abuse

But while the retaliation protections serve an important and necessary function, many management-side employment attorneys say they're also ripe for abuse by poor performers looking to inoculate themselves when they're on shaky ground.

"It's a natural place to go to protect your flank," says Fred Alvarez, the head of the employment law practice at Wilson Sonsini Goodrich & Rosati in Palo Alto, Calif.

Dealing with the situation has forced employment attorneys to come up with new plays.

"It doesn't tie your hands," says Seyfarth Shaw partner Brian Ashe of San Francisco, but it does require slowing things down.

Otherwise, it could be costly to the company.

"If you are at all precipitous in significantly disciplining the employee," Ashe says, "then you're going to buy yourself a retaliation claim that's going to be expensive."

Managers must be trained to go out of their way to thank the worker for coming forward with the allegation, writes Paul Cane Jr., a San Francisco employment partner in Paul, Hastings, Janofsky & Walker in a December 2003 article titled "When the Whistle Blows and There Is No Foul: Managing the Misguided Whistleblower."

Fighting Frivolous Claims

And any pending disciplinary actions against the whistleblower for poor performance should be subjected to de novo review [new; from the beginning] from an independent fact-finder who isn't tainted by retaliatory motivations, Cane advises. He also suggests assigning the employee a new manager that the worker gets along with.

"What in-house lawyers need to do when they have a claim is not take it lightly, and investigate these claims as vigorously as they would anything else," says Wilson, the Epstein Becker lawyer. "If they have a sexual harassment claim, for instance, we've always told in-house attorneys or HR to thoroughly investigate. The same for whistleblower claims."

Headley, the Littler Mendelson lawyer, says that if a company is large enough to have in-house counsel, it should have procedures in place to receive complaints and grievances and ensure they are screened properly—and then investigate.

"Policies are a good thing," Headley says.

But if an investigation finds no merit to the whistleblowing complaint, corporations shouldn't be fearful of getting rid of the poor-performing employee, says Jeffrey Londa, a shareholder in Ogletree, Deakins, Nash, Smoak & Stewart in Houston.

"I don't think they should be afraid to do what they otherwise would have done because [not acting] just encourages frivolous complaints," Londa says.

Higher Stakes

While employment lawyers have long helped corporate clients avoid retaliation claims involving sexual harassment and discrimination, a boom in whistleblowing has changed the rules of the game.

For one thing, the stakes are higher. The Sarbanes-Oxley Act contains both criminal and civil penalties. Section 1107 of the law imposes up to 10 years imprisonment for retaliating against an informant.

And a company's financial exposure isn't limited to fines. Reports that a company is cooking the books can have instant and disastrous consequences for its stock price.

"It raises the exposure of the claim from one plane to a complete other plane," says Wilson Sonsini's Alvarez. "The damage to the company is going to be in the market cap."

These extra considerations mean that a broader legal team is often called into action. Wilson Sonsini's Boris Feldman, a securities litigation partner in the firm's Palo Alto office, regularly pairs up with the firm's labor and employment group when whistleblower matters arise.

"From minute one it's both an HR issue and a securities law issue," says Feldman. It would be unusual, he notes, for only the employment group or the securities group to be involved.

The securities attorneys notify the company's audit committee of the allegation and spearhead an investigation to determine whether the fraud claim has any merit. In some cases, the financial investigation will even be farmed out to a separate law firm.

Changing the System

The prospects of whistleblower complaints, not to mention provisions of Sarbanes-Oxley, are forcing companies to provide an easier route for employees to bring their concerns to management.

At Houston's BMC Software Inc., for instance, senior vice president and general counsel Robert Whilden says the company set up a whistleblower hotline, as Sarbanes-Oxley suggested. Whilden says officials informed employees that complaints could stay anonymous and that he or the chairman of the board's audit committee would review the complaints initially.

Whilden says fewer than 10 complaints have come to him within the last year. Some had merit, Whilden says, but he adds none led to the discovery of a material problem.

"Some of them are even quite petty, like somebody they think is using their expense account in the wrong way, but we still investigated," he says.

For Further Discussion

1. While *The Jungle* is often accorded major historical significance as a work that changed the world, it has fared less well as a work of literature. Why do you think that this is so? (See Bloodworth, Dell, Bachelder, Rideout.)

2. The most famous scenes in *The Jungle* are those where Sinclair describes the disgusting, unsanitary conditions in the meatpacking plants. Which scenes are particularly graphic, and why do you think they have the power that they do? (See Schlosser, Denby, Arthur.)

3. Some modern critics have said that Sinclair overstates the negative conditions in the meatpacking plants and that all of the tragedies that befall Jurgis Rudkus are improbable. Do you think that *The Jungle* is too negative, or do all of the horrible events work as a story? (See Schlosser, Wade, Hitchens.)

4. According to Christopher Hitchens, despite Sinclair's distaste for the meatpacking companies' treatment of workers, he actually admires the precision, energy, and grand scale of the plants. Where do you find this fascination with the meatpacking industry in the novel? Does it overshadow or balance the negative passages, or not?

5. Some critics have criticized Jurgis's "conversion" to socialism, saying that it is improbable. Do you agree or disagree? Why? (See Rideout.)

6. The ending of *The Jungle* has been criticized as being too preachy. Even Sinclair was not happy with the unmediated socialist essay that concluded the book. How else might he have ended *The Jungle*? (See Rideout, Bachelder, Hitchens.)

7. In the original ending to *The Jungle*, Jurgis is sent to jail for his second attack on Connor. In a short paragraph that begins right after "CHICAGO WILL BE OURS!" Sinclair writes: "All of which was at one o'clock on the morning of the day after election; and at one o'clock of the afternoon of the same day Jurgis was handcuffed to a detective, and on his way to serve a two years' sentence in state's prison for assault with intent to kill." Why do you think Sinclair omitted this part in later editions?

For Further Reading

Charles Dickens *Hard Times.* London: Bradbury & Evans, 1854.

Benjamin Disraeli *Sybil, or the Two Nations.* London: Henry Colburn, 1845.

John Dos Passos *The 42nd Parallel.* New York, London: Harper & Brothers, 1930.

John Dos Passos *1919.* New York: Harcourt Brace, 1932.

John Dos Passos *The Big Money.* New York: Harcourt Brace, 1936.

Frank Norris *The Octopus.* New York: Doubleday, Page, 1901.

George Orwell *Animal Farm.* London: Secker & Warburg, 1945.

Upton Sinclair *Boston: A Novel.* New York: Albert & Charles Boni, 1928.

Upton Sinclair *King Coal: A Novel.* New York: Macmillan, 1918.

Upton Sinclair *Oil!* New York: Alfred & Charles Boni, 1927.

John Steinbeck *The Grapes of Wrath.* New York: Viking, 1939.

Mary Heaton Vorse *Strike!* New York: Horace Liveright, 1930.

Bibliography

Books

Daniel Aaron   *Writers on the Left*. New York: Avon, 1969.

Stanley Aronowitz   *False Promises: The Shaping of American Working Class Consciousness*. New York: McGraw-Hill, 1973.

Abraham Blinderman   *Critics on Upton Sinclair: Readings in Literary Criticism*. Coral Gables, FL: University of Miami Press, 1975.

William A Bloodworth Jr.   *Upton Sinclair*. Boston: Twayne, 1971.

Harold Bloom   *Upton Sinclair's "The Jungle"*. Modern critical interpretations. Philadelphia: Chelsea House, 2002.

David Brody   *Workers in Industrial America: Essays on the Twentieth-Century Struggle*. New York: Oxford University Press, 1980.

David Mark Chalmers   *The Social and Political Ideas of the Muckrakers*. New York: Citadel, 1964.

Scott Derks   *Working Americans, 1880–2005*. Lakeville, CT: Grey House, 2000.

Foster Rhea Dulles   *Labor in America: A History*. New York: Crowell, 1966.

Dieter Herms, ed.   *Upton Sinclair: Literature and Social Reform.* Frankfurt: Peter Lang, 1990.

Nelson Lichtenstein   *State of the Union: A Century of American Labor; Politics and Society in Twentieth-Century America.* Princeton, NJ: Princeton University Press, 2002.

Greg Mitchell   *The Campaign of the Century: Upton Sinclair's Race for Governor of California and the Birth of Media Politics.* New York: Random House, 1992.

David Montgomery   *The Fall of the House of Labor: The Workplace, the State, and American Labor Activism, 1865–1925.* Cambridge: Cambridge University Press, 1987.

R.N. Mookerjee   *Art for Social Justice: The Major Novels of Upton Sinclair.* Metuchen, NJ: Scarecrow, 1988.

Priscilla Murolo and A.B. Chitty   *From the Folks Who Brought You the Weekend: A Short, Illustrated History of Labor in the United States.* New York: New Press, 2001.

Ivan Scott   *Upton Sinclair: The Forgotten Socialist.* Lanham, MD: University Press of America, 1996.

Periodicals

Ed Ainsworth   "Remembering 'Uppie,'" *Saturday Review of Literature.* September 30, 1967.

David Bacon   "Labor Needs a Radical Vision," *Colorlines Magazine*, Fall 2005.

George Becker   "Upton Sinclair: Quixote in a Flivver," *College English*, December 1959.

Hugh J. Dawson   "Winston Churchill and Upton Sinclair: An Early Review of *The Jungle*," *American Literary Realism, 1870–1910*, Fall 1991.

James C. Duram   "Upton Sinclair's Realistic Romanticism," *University Studies*, May 1970.

Granville Hicks   "The Survival of Upton Sinclair," *College English*, January 1943.

J.D. Koemer   "The Last of the Muckrake Men," *South Atlantic Quarterly*, April 1956.

Marcel van der Linden   "The 'Globalization' of Labor and Working-Class History and Its Consequences," *International Labor and Working Class History*, vol. 65 (2004).

Angie C. Marek   "The Laborer's Lot," *U.S. News & World Report*, Sept 22, 2003.

Matthew J. Morris   "The Two Lives of Jurgis Rudkus," *American Literary Realism, 1870–1910*, Winter 1997.

Howard H. Quint   "Upton Sinclair's Quest for Artistic Independence—1909," *American Literature*, May 1957.

Chivy Sok   "What Is Child Labor?" *Faces: People, Places, and Cultures*, April 2006.

Harvey Swandos "The World of Upton Sinclair," *Atlantic Monthly*, December 1961.

JoAnn Wypijewski "The Days of Bread and Roses: In a Time When Most Americans Feel Only a Paycheck Away from Disaster, Can Unions Rouse Beyond Their Ranks?" *Mother Jones*, July/August 2005.

Index